MONTGOMERY
COUNTY
GHOST
STORIES

CHARLES J. ADAMS III

EXETER HOUSE BOOKS
2000

Montgomery County Ghost Stories

Published by EXETER HOUSE BOOKS

Exeter House Books
PO Box 8134
Reading, PA 19603

ISBN 1-880683-14-8

First Edition
June 2000
Printed in the United States of America

All photographs by the author unless otherwise noted.
All post cards from the collection of the author.

To Muffy

TABLE OF CONTENTS

MONTGOMERY COUNTY GHOST STORIES

Introduction

There exists in Montgomery County an odd and sometimes uncomfortable admixture of old and new, bold and subdued, quaint and contemporary.

It is a sprawling county in which myriad cultures mix in a stewpot of customs, traditions, and superstitions.

It is a county with corners of early Quaker, Mennonite and Pennsylvania German influences, and where the cash crops of the land range from hay and corn to houses and condos.

It is where George Washington's army suffered through the winter of 1777 at Valley Forge and where tourists and conventioneers relax in comfort a stone's throw from where the army's crude cabins once stood.

It is where major pharmaceutical manufacturers coexist with major farm product processors.

It is where at one place a "hotel" has a concierge, room service and a pool while at another place "hotel" means a bartender, a waitress, and a pool table or two.

In Montgomery County, historic sites abut high-rises, superhighways parallel gravel lanes, and the promise of progress rubs shoulders with the pride of the past.

Look at any road map of Pennsylvania and you will see that the shaded portions that define the "metropolitan area" of suburban Philadelphia extends through two-thirds of Montgomery County.

And, peruse the roster of school districts in Montgomery County and you will find that one–Abington– calls its sports teams the *Ghosts*. Even if that nickname was adopted after a visit to an Abington pep rally by football legend Red "The Galloping Ghost" Grange, it is still interesting that Abington, in Montgomery County, is one of the few schools in the country with *Ghosts* on its playing fields and courts.

To tally and tell the stories of the supernatural in this book was a daunting task.

So rich in history is this county that to claim that this slim volume is a complete collection of such stories would be folly.

But through electronic mail, telephone calls, endless hours in libraries and historical societies, and in person-to-person interviews, we have attempted to chronicle and present at least a cross-section of the most inexplicable and, we hope, interesting and entertaining stories.

What you are about to read is true—at least as true as the quotations from past accounts and present eyewitnesses can be.

Little has been embellished.

Little had to be.

Montgomery County is a complicated county, if you let it be. But between those highways and beyond those housing developments is a land where legends still cling to life within the ledgers of those who care, and where strange stories still circulate among those Montgomery Countians who have been held in the grip...of ghosts.

Charles J. Adams III
June, 2000

MONTGOMERY COUNTY GHOST STORIES

Foreword

*The histories of Montgomery County have nothing to
say about the ghosts and the haunted houses of this region.
Nor has any local historian ever
written a paper on this subject.
Yet, it is capable of being developed into a most
interesting chapter–nay, perhaps, into a book.*

Those words are from a newspaper article that was
discovered in a scrapbook deep in the files of the Historical
Society of Montgomery County.

The names of the writer and the publication were not
retrievable.

The date, though, was December, 1925.

And now, 75 years later, this is the book–the first
compilation of ghost stories from within the 483 square
miles of the third most populous county in Pennsylvania.

It should be noted that the above 1925 quotation was
not entirely accurate.

In his 1884 *History of Montgomery County,* Theodore W.
Bean did refer to ghosts in the chapter, "Local
Superstitions."

Bean recalled old tales of witches and witch doctors
(referring specifically to one in Flourtown and another in
Upper Dublin), and actually presented a lengthy
dissertation on 18th and early 19th century hauntings.

From Bean, we quote:

*A belief in ghosts or spooks was prevalent. To conceal ill-
gotten gain or treasure would cause the spirit of the perpetrator
to guard it after his death. Indian ghosts, it was said, haunted
places where the natural scenery was likely to engender such*

feelings as gloomy forests and deep solitary glens by running streams.

The Perkiomen, with its numerous branches, and the Pennypack particularly were believed to be thus frequented, and where the spirits by their graves kept vigils.

Deserted houses, old limekilns and secluded graveyards and places where unnatural deaths had occurred or suicide committed would be avoided at night as suspicious places. Eyewitnesses of undoubted veracity have informed us of seeing on dark nights lights in graveyards.....

Bean then presented a litany of superstitions, omens, and harbingers–traditions and superstitions brought to Montgomery County by the diverse array of immigrants who settled it.

And, throughout later writings on a variety of levels, the notion of ghosts continued to surface.

But, it is truly ironic that any self-respecting scribe such as that 1925 newspaper writer would make a statement as broad as he or she did.

Very soon, you will read a story that will confirm that indeed, Montgomery County's ghost stories were given their just due quite early on–*quite* early.

More on that later.

In the waning years of the 20th century, ghosts and haunted places seemed to rise in prominence and respectability in Montgomery County.

The Valley Forge Convention and Visitors Bureau published a special "Historic Haunts" section within its tourists' guide. Several historic sites in the county presented Halloween programs that mentioned their own hauntings.

The Morgan Log House in Towamencin, whose staff claimed no resident wraiths when contacted by the researchers for this volume, did, however, hold a program in 1997 in which "...costumed historical interpreters show how the early Welsh used plants to ward off 'evil spirits' and summoned ghosts to foretell the future."

MONTGOMERY COUNTY GHOST STORIES

Too often, though, to discover any of these tales, one had to veer far off the beaten path of "the norm" and chart an unfamiliar and uncomfortable itinerary.

In life, there are those courses that we may follow which will lead us along broad, well-lit and well-traveled boulevards of history.

And, there are those folks who prefer never to wander far from that secure way.

But, as you have chosen this volume, you are among those who are willing to break away from the pack.

Let us, then, stray from the course where the signs are bright and the directions are clear.

Follow, please, as we steer away from the avenues of reality and find the dark roads and even darker lanes that lead to places few choose to go.

In the following pages you will discover ghost stories told in olden times, as well as ghost stories told by people you may know about places to which you may go.

We will begin this journey with an old story–the very oldest possible, in fact.

Yes, the first story in the first chapter in our *Montgomery County Ghost Stories* has actually been acknowledged as being the first recorded ghost story ever in America.

The Zieber-Schwenk Burial Ground, site of
"America's First Ghost Story"

Susanna's Ghost

Susanna Reimer could be considered to be a part of American history.

It is believed that she was the first person in the American colonies to see and talk about a ghost, and then have it recorded for others to read.

Susanna Reimer is one important character in what could truly be called "America's First Ghost Story."

Susanna's father, Frederick Reimer (a.k.a. Fritz Reymer), had come to the county in 1730 from Germany. Almost immediately upon settling along the Scioto (a.k.a. Society and/or Sciota) Creek in what is now Upper Frederick Township, he became active in church affairs and took his place as a respected member of the growing frontier community in what was then a wide area known generally as Falkner Swamp.

He would have no idea that eight years after his arrival

in the New World, an event would take place that would etch his, and his daughter's names in the history books.

It was in the middle of August, 1738–just another day on the farm for nine-year old Susanna Reimer. She and her sister, Elizabeth, were finishing their morning chores when something caught Susanna's attention.

A stranger–a tall, rugged stranger with a long mustache drooping around his lips–was sitting on a stump in the farmyard. Quietly, alone, and sitting as if he was oblivious to his human observer, the chap seemed agitated, as Susanna would later say.

At first, Susanna had no reason to suspect what she was seeing was of a spectral nature. For all intents, the man was nothing more than a wanderer who had come to call.

And yet, when Susanna pointed the man out to her sister, Elizabeth responded with confounded confusion. She had seen nothing, no one.

Indeed, as Susanna glanced again toward the stump, the gent was gone. She scratched her head as if to doubt her own initial sighting. Maybe she had imagined the man. Maybe he had stealthily gone away. No matter what, she told Elizabeth that she must have been mistaken and kept her odd vision to herself.

Not much later that day, Susanna was alone as she passed a neighbor's house–Johannes Zieber's–when she saw the same man again. This time, he was standing unobtrusively next to one of Zieber's farmhands in the garden. As Susanna watched, she could tell that the farmhand had no idea a man–or a *ghost*–was standing right next to him.

Within a few minutes, the man left the farmhand's side and walked from the garden into a wheat field. As he walked, Susanna believed, he seemed to leave the wheat totally undisturbed. Eventually, he disappeared into the field.

Now the little girl became even more confused and, perhaps, a bit concerned.

7

Still, there was no reason for her to believe that this mysterious stranger was anything but that. Certainly, she would eventually meet this visitor and the mystery would be solved.

Sure enough, she would meet the visitor a third time. This time, she would speak to the man. He would respond. And, their conversation would echo through the ages.

On that third and fateful encounter, Susanna was strolling through another part of the farm when she spied the mustachioed man straddling the peak of a thatched-roof stable.

She watched in utter amazement as the man furiously pulled large wads of thatching from the roof. Angrily he yanked the material from the roof and tossed it to the ground.

But, Susanna quickly noticed that as the man pulled the thatching from the roof, no hole appeared in the roof. As he tossed the straw from the roof, no pile appeared on the ground. It seemed to vanish as it fell.

For several minutes, Susanna watched in wide-eyed amazement. Transfixed as she was on the man, it seemed as if he was, literally and figuratively, in his own world. He paid no attention whatsoever to Susanna, and never once acknowledged her existence.

The little girl had seen enough. She ran back to her house and summoned the oldest of her eight sisters. With that 17-year old sibling she returned to the stable and the straw-slinging man.

As they arrived at the outbuilding, Susanna fully expected her sister to stand back in amazement as the two shared the sight. This time, the man was inside the stable, looking out a barn door.

But alas, her sister saw nothing. Susanna alone would see him once again.

Either in condescending jest or with sincerity, the older girl urged Susanna to "talk to the man." "Ask him who he is, and what he's doing," she told Susanna. "Then," the 17-year old instructed, "tell me what he tells you."

8

MONTGOMERY COUNTY GHOST STORIES

And, Susanna did so.

It was then when Susanna realized for the first time that the man who appeared first on the stump, then standing next to a farmhand, and later madly flinging phantom straw from the stable roof...was a ghost.

As Susanna asked her first question, the man on the roof stopped thrashing in the thatching and gazed down sternly at the nervous little girl. With a booming but somehow hollow voice, he offered cryptic answers.

While he never identified himself, he told Susanna that he had been waiting for her–or for any human–to see him and speak to him.

"Now," he bellowed, "with your help, I can be released!"

He went on to explain that he had departed life with an unpaid debt remaining on his conscience. Until that matter was settled, he said, he could never rest in peace.

Susanna felt as if it was becoming quite painful for the man to speak. His voice weakened and became scratchy with every sentence he spoke.

He told Susanna how he had died suddenly, how the debt–owed to a Dutch woman named "Steinmann"–had been his last mortal thought, and how he could only appear to certain human beings and only for short periods of time.

Within Susanna's conversation with the ghost, he told her that, for whatever reasons, he could not expect his widow to repay what he said was "50 guldens" to the "Steinmann" woman. That's the way it would be, he said. His wife could never assume the debt.

After conferring with her older sister, Susanna told the spirit that she would do all she could to make sure the debt would be paid. It was with that pledge that the very countenance of the ghost seemed to change. He seemed more content.

With that, he told Susanna that he must return to what he described as his "home."

Now, fully suspecting that she was actually talking to a ghost, Susanna was compelled to ask him where "home"

9

was.

He pointed toward a simple cemetery down by a tree line next to the creek. "There," he told her.

He then turned and walked to the graveyard. He had taken only a few steps inside the low fence before he disappeared near a short tombstone.

It was the Zieber family burial ground, and it was the man's eternal "home."

Susanna and Elizabeth Reimer agreed that their parents should be apprised of the strange séances.

Both further agreed that the man would not have, nor could have, done them harm, and concurred that Susanna had really been speaking with a resident of "the other side."

They also realized that convincing their parents of any of this might be a tough task.

Still, they told their father, Frederick Reimer, of their encounters.

He listened with fascination and never once doubted his darling daughter's veracity.

He also agreed to do everything he could to find the "Steinmann" woman and pay her, as long as it would put the man's spirit to rest.

As the story played out, several interesting facts came to light.

When the girls directed their father to the Zieber burial ground and the tombstone at which the ghost vanished, they discovered it was the grave marked with the name of a man known only as "Miller."

Not much was known about the man.

Some neighbors who were told of the Reimer girls' experiences recalled that the "Miller" man did odd jobs around the area and had died about four years back.

And, incredibly, they remembered that his stock in trade was *roof thatching*.

A bit later, Miller's widow was found.

She told the Reimers that she remembered that although her husband had asked to borrow the money from the woman she called Katherine Steinmann, the woman refused his request.

Her husband and Mrs. Steinmann argued over the loan arrangement and–according to one account–Mrs. Steinmann became so upset with Miller that she placed a curse on him.

More research was done on several fronts. It was discovered that on the British brig "Hope," which docked in Philadelphia in August, 1733, there was a couple by the names of Hans and Katherine Steinmann and several families named Miller. No one, not the little girl, her father, or the neighbors, could have known that.

The story spread far and wide, and ten years later became an international sensation.

The noted Germantown printer Christopher Saur (a.k.a. Sower, Sauer), probably best known for producing the second bible ever printed in America in 1743, got wind of the story and printed it in his newspaper and in a small book, *Erscheinungen der Geister*, or *The Appearances of Ghosts*.

That story was then picked up by a German magazine, *Spiritual Reports*.

In all of those publications, in America and Europe, an appeal was made for Catherine Steinmann to contact the Reimers so "Miller's" debt could be repaid and his spirit could rest peacefully.

Mrs. Steinmann never surfaced. The loan, if there really ever was one, was never paid.

And Miller's ghost was never heard from again.

Or, was it?

A tragedy on Christmas night, 1757, punctuated this ghost story when Frederick Reimer was found frozen to death in the snow on his farm.

It was believed by many neighbors that Reimer's mysterious death really was related to tale told by his daughter.

While Reimer and others had tried valiantly to find the Dutch woman and retire Miller's debt, Miller's ghost was never appeased. This, after it had been assured by little Susanna Reimer that the matter would be resolved.

The superstitious folks up Falkner Swamp way soon

spread word that Miller's restless and vindictive spirit vented its frustration on Frederick Reimer that Christmas.

They said his ghost rose one more time from his grave and sent Reimer's remains deep into the same soil Miller called "home."

The bramble-strangled Zieber-Schwenk Burial Ground is within private property along Faust Road in Upper Frederick Township. Trying to find it is not recommended. Trespassers are not tolerated. One of the oldest graveyards in western Montgomery County, the plot is believed to hold 200 bodies, including that of George Schwenk, founder of Schwenksville. Few tombstones are visible these days, with most reduced to stony stubs. It is from here that the ghost called "Miller" rose to visit Susanna Reimer. At the time of the publication of this book the owner of the property on which the Reimer farm and this graveyard are located was Mrs. Joseph Kwapisz, who told us that she has encountered a ghostly figure she described as "A little old lady wearing a shawl" wandering through her home. "It could have been an optical illusion," she said. "But I don't know why people are worried about ghosts–they don't bother anybody."

The Peter Wentz Farmstead, Worcester

Phantom Footsteps in History

This is a story about a ghost which is said to dwell within a Philadelphia historic site.

What, you ask? What does a Philadelphia ghost have to do with Montgomery County?

Although deep in Montgomery County, the Peter Wentz Farmstead is indeed a part of Philadelphia's history.

When the Wentz family settled near what is now the village of Worcester, their spread was located in what was then Philadelphia County. At that time, the boundaries of Philadelphia extended diagonally from its present site on the Delaware River into the frontier along the Blue Mountain ridge.

The influence of Philadelphia can be seen throughout the architectural and furniture styles of the Wentz farm, and throughout the place there are a few surprises–including a ghost or two.

The Wentz family settled in Penn's Wood from Switzerland and surrounding areas. Peter Wentz Sr. was,

13

in legend, a flamboyant sailor who commanded a privateer on the high seas and collected enough booty to buy thousands of acres in what are now Berks, Lehigh, and Montgomery counties.

Wentz's interests expanded from farming to mining, and his property became a showplace of the region.

The farm which is now open to the public as an historic site was built by Peter Wentz Jr., and he and his family occupied it during its most productive and historically significant years.

In terms of longevity, the land should more properly be called the Shultz Farm, since that family bought it from the Wentzes in the late-18th century and lived on it for 175 years.

It was in 1969 when the Montgomery County Commissioners, urged on and advised by county historical advocates, purchased the 1758 Georgian-style home, outbuildings, and land and ordered its complete restoration.

When the farmstead was unveiled to the public in 1976, it took its place as a sparkling gem in the state's dazzling jewelry box of history. It has since been called one of the three best historical restorations in the state.

What set it aside is its architectural, decorative, and historical importance. Historically, it is where George Washington visited on two occasions in 1777. The general planned his strategies for the Battle of Germantown in a second-floor room, and retired to the Wentz home following that battle.

Architecturally, the farmstead is remarkable, from the snake fence that surrounds it to the startling wall decorations that are repeated in nearly every room and corridor of the home.

Although Georgian—and thus English in style, the features of the residence are quite Germanic, reflecting the Wentz family traditions.

Some of those features have proven to be striking not only to those who view them casually but also to certain experts in the field of historical preservation and restoration.

The most obvious and arguably most controversial is the recurring theme of sponged splotches of black dots on the kitchen walls and the dots, crescents, and stripes on the dadoes in all but the dining room.

While the original wall paint schemes are long faded and covered over, a specialist in historic paint, during the restoration process, discovered incontrovertibly, that these unusual patterns were on the walls of the mid-1700s Wentz house.

Anyone who expects quaint, typically Colonial paint schemes will have to look at the woodwork and upper walls for that. Otherwise, the wall decor seems more 1960s Psychedelic than 1760s Colonial.

Peculiar, too, is the positioning of the fireplace in the winter kitchen. It is backed against an inner wall, thus enabling the placement of a five-plate stove in the adjoining dining room. That, then, doubles the heat-giving capacity of the hearth.

One must look in every corner and along every surface for the intricacies of the Wentz house's interior. Some of the beams contain elaborate carvings and the brick pattern on the summer kitchen and breezeway floors are unique.

Unique, as well, is the breezeway itself. It is not typical of homes of that time and that place. Neither is the window seat in the living room.

These splendid features could well go unnoticed to those who marvel more in the fine antique furnishings. To those folks, the Peter Wentz house is a treasure trove.

The furniture is based on a 1794 inventory of Wentz's possessions, and much of it is excellent craftsmanship by any number of noted Philadelphia manufacturers.

The rooms are also peppered with high-quality utensils and accessories of English and American origin, including a copper teakettle from the forge of John Babb of Reading.

Near the farmhouse is an 18th century, raised-bed garden, and a barn which actually predates the house by some 14 years.

The barn served the original Wentz farmhouse, which was built in 1744. It was a relatively simple, three-room building which was replaced by a mill. Both structures have virtually disappeared.

There is, however, evidence of the foundations of those earlier buildings, and architectural work continues on those sites.

Beyond the historical and architectural wonders of the property, however, are the less visible and more elusive qualities of the Peter Wentz Farmstead.

The ghosts.

For that story, we went to no less an authority than Elizabeth R. Gamon, the administrator of the property.

Her involvement at Peter Wentz Farmstead began as a volunteer when the county purchased the site. Few, if any, individuals know the farmstead as intimately as Mrs. Gamon.

So, when she speaks of ghostly activity in the old farmhouse, people listen.

"I have experienced a being here at the site several times," Mrs. Gamon said as our investigative team met with her and her assistant, Philip Nord.

As she and the authors sat at a table in a room just outside Mrs. Gamon's office on the second floor of the reception center, she continued.

"My personal feeling is that it's a female, but I don't know for sure.

"I have heard, while in the breezeway, footsteps above me in the loft. This has been while I have been in the house by myself, at a quiet time of the day."

But, Mrs. Gamon maintained that the loft is not the only area the phantom footfalls can be heard.

"I have also heard, several times when I was on the first floor, footsteps crossing the second floor. It is always under the same set of circumstances; quiet, no one around, just me.

"I'd go upstairs to check...nothing."

16

Could it have been the wind? Squirrels or mice?

"No," Mrs. Gamon insisted. "I'm convinced we have someone here."

The height of the ghostly activity was during the months and years following the restoration.

"It was when the house was being disturbed," she continued. "I wonder if it was because we disturbed the site that the activity took place. Did we disturb whatever was in the house at that time?"

Indeed, there are those paranormal researchers who would agree that Mrs. Gamon hit the psychic nail on the head—literally and figuratively.

Allow me to introduce what I call the "rusty nail theory" of ghostly energy. It is a premise subscribed to by many observers, and a concept I have put forth in previous books.

Upon death, I suggest, what was flesh and bone may become dust.   But, what were electrical charges in the nervous system may continue as information-laden impulses which stay suspended and circulating in an eternal swirl of a magnetic field.

Could these impulses—these shards of emotions and information leftover from a life—then record themselves somehow, on something?

As in simple video or audio recording, could not these invisible impulses become attracted to and deposited on ferrous oxide—rust?

Could these scientifically rational and conceivable electrical charges which burst from the corporeal confines at the time of extreme trauma—including, but not limited to, death, be the seeds of the supernatural?

Could these bits and pieces be ghosts?

If there is one thread which weaves its way through the majority of tales I have investigated, it is that on virtually every "case" the building in which the haunting took or is taking place has been renovated or altered in some way.

Could the renovations have disturbed that recording by exposing the rust and allowing an unwary psychic mind—

such as, in this case, Mrs. Gamon's–to push the "playback" button and detect those impulses?

As inconceivable as this may be to some, so is the proposition that living faces and forms and voices and sounds could be recorded on strips of rust-coated plastic and retrieved on a glass screen or paper speaker.

But those are the wonders we call audio and video, which in an electronic age seem all so natural.

And when things go bump in the night within the walls of a proud, old building, the answers to seemingly unanswerable questions may very well be as scientific as they are psychic.

The pages of history do not disclose all the answers regarding the drama and trauma which must have played out inside the walls of the Wentz house.

"Not really," added Mrs. Gamon. "There was a lot of disturbance during the Revolutionary War when the general was in residence.

"We have reason to believe that some of the Revolutionary War soldiers were buried on the site, so I'm sure there was trauma that took place in that time."

Still, Mrs. Gamon believed her unseen resident is a female.

"It's just listening to those footsteps. It was not a heavy footstep, it was very light," she said.

"I don't think she's any threat. I don't think she was here in anger, or anything," she added.

Perhaps now that the farmstead has settled into its role as an historic site, the ghost itself has settled down a bit.

But others have heard the footsteps, and at least one theory has been offered regarding possible circumstances which could serve as a baseline for the restless soul on the upper floor.

"We have found, in the attic, traces where there had been partitions, as though it had been divided into smaller rooms at one time," Mrs. Gamon said.

"And, we wonder if, perhaps, at some time during this

18

building's existence, whether it was in the 18th or 19th centuries, they had housed, perhaps, a disturbed individual up there and had to lock the area.

"Now, this is not the impression I got with the sounds I heard. I think that would be a more anxious, agitated type, and what I heard and feel was not."

Philip Nord added his thoughts on the matter. "It's not a scary house," he said. "It's a happy house. There are certain feelings in the rooms, and I think you have to emotionally be in tune with that. And, I think the people who have experienced things there have a certain sense—and not everyone has that ability to feel that somebody, or something, is there.

"We've had 300 years of life and death at this house," he proffered, "and several wars, as well."

But, there's more—much more to this story.

"We do have one thing," Mrs. Gamon said, almost as an afterthought. "We have a photograph.

"It was taken by our first administrator, who happened to be my husband [Albert T. Gamon].

"It was a photo taken to be used as a Christmas card for our volunteers.

"There was no individual in that scene. But there was a shadow of what looks like a person. Everyone who has seen it says it's a person. For years we said that has to be another being. But, we know it wasn't a living being!"

Interpretation of that photograph aside, Mrs. Gamon speaks affectionately of the Wentz farm—of its history and its hauntings—as if it were her own property. It is not, of course. It belongs to Montgomery County, and thus all Montgomery Countians.

But there is one property that Mrs. Gamon can discuss with unqualified authority—her own circa 1735 house near Zieglerville.

And yes, within its walls odd occurrences have taken place since she and her family moved there in 1958.

"The house was added onto in 1799 and also in the 20th century," she said. "In that original 1735 section, on

19

the second floor, which was my sons' bedroom, for the years during their active years of growing up, I would go up in the evening, turn the lights on, turn their beds down, go back downstairs, have dinner, and go back up to put them to bed.

"The bed would be remade. The lights would be turned off. There was no one up there, or in the house!

"Now, to further emphasize this, we raised English Pointers, and we had several in the house over the years. Not one of those dogs would go into that bedroom. They would get to the top of the steps and freeze *en pointe*. They would not go into that room."

Did she believe the tidying up was the act of an invisible, ethereal house guest? What was her initial response?

"Confusion," she said. "Now, it didn't happen every day, but looking back on it, my husband noted that it seemed to take place during very active periods in our lives. I feel that it was a friendly ghost, but it somehow didn't like what we were doing in that room."

"Ye Olde Grist Mill".
Ardmore, Pa. Built 1746.

The Roberts Mill, as seen in a ca. 1905 post card.

The Fiend of the Mill: Myth & Reality

Strange tales abound in Montgomery County–tales which have survived the centuries in their telling and retelling. Stories first told by those who were present at the very time and at the very source of whatever smidgen of truth may have ever existed. Stories which have become legends.

One such tale is that of the ghost at Glen Willow, described in an old account as a village along Mill Creek near its confluence with the Schuylkill River.

"The tiny village...consists of some twenty straggling cottages, a flour mill, and quite a number of ancient ruins dating from days prior to the Revolution. One building which has been recently renovated bears upon its gable end the date '1690.'"

The words are from an 1899 edition of *the Philadelphia Inquirer,* and they are beneath the headline:

"GHOSTS IN THE MILL."

The story about that old mill continues: "It has a

history, dark with the murder of many of the brave
American soldiers of the Revolution.

"It is credited with a ghost, and it still owns all that is
left of the 'grist mill' where the fiendish Englishman George
Roberts, and his slave ground up glass with corn and gave it
to the men of George Washington's army, to work its cruel
havoc among those English bullets failed to slay."

Heady historical stuff, eh? But, is it entirely accurate?

This, we shall soon explore.

The article included an interview with one "James
Carr", who was described as "probably the oldest living
man in all the valley."

Carr spun the yarns his father and his father's father
had told him–yarns about the evil deeds said to have been
carried out by George Roberts in the old mill.

Roberts was said to have come from England to
Philadelphia, and then to the mill site along Mill Creek and
the Schuylkill River.

The mill did brisk business selling its flour to the troops
stationed at Valley Forge and other points around
Philadelphia. But soon, very horrible events played out
among the soldiers.

"It was discovered that every man who ate bread made
from Roberts' flour was taken with frightful convulsions
and eventually died," James Carr told the *Inquirer*.

"Very soon," James Carr said, "it was discovered that
there was kept in the mill yard quantities of broken glass for
no apparent purpose whatsoever.

"Then, Roberts was found to receive suspicious visitors
who, on being tracked, were found to be spies from the
British. A little further investigation resulted in the
discovery of the purpose to which the glass was put.

"This fiend and his black partner were passing it
between the millstones and grinding it up with the corn!"

Shortly after the grisly discovery, with local sentiment
building to a lynch mob mentality, George Roberts, they say,
took the coward's way out.

A band of vigilantes surrounded the mill one night,

hoping to capture Roberts and make him pay for his crime.

"But," Carr recalled, "when the mill was broken into, Roberts was found hanging by the neck to a beam, as cold and dead as one of his own millstones."

Roberts' collaborator was taken into custody and nearly hanged until he convinced his captors that he was a slave, and thus an unwilling partner in the fatal scheme.

The posse allowed the slave to leave, but promptly put a torch to the old mill.

And, that mill at Glen Willow rapidly took on the reputation as being haunted.

James Carr heard those tales, and acknowledged that strange things would be seen and heard amid the ruins and later restoration of the mill.

So, where is that mill today? Does the ghost of the fiendish miller still roam the land, no matter what is built upon it now?

More than that, did a fiendish miller ever roam that land? And, where exactly is that land?

Therein lies one of Lower Merion Township's most enduring–and downright confusing–mysteries.

You know the game, "Whisper Down the Alley"–in which the salient facts of a story become twisted as the story is whispered from person to person?

Well, in the case of the "George Roberts" and his mill, the "alley" is long and the whispers have been plentiful.

To begin with, despite the expected credibility of the 1899 *Inquirer* article, the very existence of a "George Roberts" as relates to the "ground glass" incident is in doubt.

Furthermore, there may never have been any such "ground glass" incident; nor was there any suicide or contrite slave. Or, the "ground glass" mill might have been somewhere else altogether.

But, there is a ghost–keep reading.

To illustrate the confusion which has circulated around this story for the last couple centuries or so, allow me to cite a sepia tone German post card of around 1900 which depicts the "Ruins of Mill where glass was ground in the flour....". It is placed at Gulph Mill, near Conshohocken.

There's another English "Tuck's" post card of about the same vintage which does not mention the "ground glass" incident, but displays the same mill ruins at Gulf (sic) Mill, Valley Forge, Pa.

And then, there's a mid-1960s *Main Line Times* article which reaffirmed the Roberts Mill as the "ground glass" mill. And, the article continued, "On the opposite side of the road [from the mill] stands the house where the Tory miller lived. It has been known as the Haunted House as far back as anyone remembers. The Haunted House was a deserted ruin up to 1901."

Those elements were corrected a week later by Mrs. John Waltz and Mrs. Joseph Collopy, who said the "haunted" house was not where the initial article stated.

Both women recalled from their childhoods stories of the Roberts house being haunted. Mrs. Waltz spoke of folks coming by to see the tree from which Roberts was hanged–and find the openings of tunnels which supposedly ran through the soil of the mill property.

Tunnels? A "Hanging Tree?" The plot thickens!

Consider another *Main Line Times* article in June, 1980, in which the whispers in the alley took many more bizarre turns.

The writer of the "Actual Story of John Roberts" stated that Roberts was rousted by American troops and "fled through a tunnel in alarm, mounted a horse in pitch darkness and galloped away."

Roberts' sons, the story continued, barricaded the door to facilitate their father's escape. But, one of the sons took a bullet and was wounded as the troops "led by Col. Isaac Potter, swinging his sword with vigor," barged in and seized the mill.

That account further stated that a couple days later, a gang of neighbors descended on the Roberts mill after they were told about the "ground glass" affair.

Of course, they didn't find the "fiendish miller," Roberts, but they did find an apparently innocent millhand, a German immigrant named Fishburn.

It was Fishburn who was lynched on an apple tree in an orchard next to the Roberts house. It would thus be Fishburn's ghost that may haunt the property.

Or would it?

Another piece in the *Main Line Times* feature four years later read: "People used to say that Roberts was hanged in the orchard..."

What's more, "According to legend, the body was buried under a slab in the cellar and his ghost haunted both the house and the orchard."

The story has been bandied about in various media for the last several decades, and every version, no matter how sincere or seemingly authoritative, has caused more babble in this particular legend's alley.

Interestingly, one of those newspaper articles mentioned that the notion of the tunnels on the Roberts property so intrigued folks that even "Gov. Isaac Pennypacker undertook to search for the tunnel with a lantern."

There never was a Gov. Isaac Pennypacker. At least, never in Pennsylvania. However, there was a Gov. Samuel Pennypacker. And, that governor did have a deep interest in folklore, legends, and ghosts of Montgomery County, as you shall discover elsewhere in this book.

One would hope that the latest information available about the convoluted, complicated George Roberts/ground glass/slave/tunnels/hanging tree/Fishburn lynching story might help to silence the whispering.

Perhaps it will.

For that information, we turn to *The First 300: The Amazing and Rich History of Lower Merion*, a superb volume published in 2000 by The Lower Merion Historical Society (Diane Publishing Co.).

In it are five full pages dedicated to the Roberts Mill. The John Roberts Mill. More specifically, the John Roberts III Mill.

Roberts III inherited the mill from Roberts II who inherited it from Roberts I who was a Welsh immigrant in the late 17th century. "No documentation has been found," the account in the book discloses, "of Roberts's exact arrival to his land, what his first buildings were or where they were located."

But, there is much known about Roberts III's property. On his estimated 700 acres were orchards, meadows, and mills which pumped out paper, lumber, gunpowder, and flour.

But, never a hint of ground glass in that flour.

In fact, under the heading of "Fiction, Not Fact," the article debunks several previously-mentioned myths.

•Roberts was not hanged by an irate mob in his yard. Neither did a mob, unable to find him, hang a worker there.

•Roberts was not buried beneath a hanging tree, but in the cemetery at Merion Meeting.

•Roberts did not escape through a tunnel from the cellar.

•Roberts did not add ground glass to flour meant for American soldiers.

The history of the mill, and especially the 1752 home built to house Jane and John Roberts III, follows the story through and including Roberts' execution in Philadelphia on November 4, 1778–a "political murder," as some have called it.

And, the article includes another sidebar entitled: "Haunted House?"

Notice the question mark which indicates some doubt?

In search of answers to those doubts, we spoke with the charming Christine Jones, who should know something about the haunting of the Roberts house.

Mrs. Jones and her husband Dick reside in the John Roberts house.

And, her first words as we sat at a table in the Lower Merion Historical Society library at the Ashbridge House in Rosemont were, "It's often called the John Roberts *haunted* house."

It's a moniker she has no problems with whatsoever.

When the Joneses moved into the house, Christine was "thrilled" to learn that it was within a local and state historic district and on the National Register of Historic Places.

Although not a trained historian, she immediately plunged into a personal project which would verify, authenticate, and alter certain historical fables or facts

27

about the place.

What she *was,* was a trained and skilled decorator. And, she turned the 1752 structure into a showpiece home as she and her husband became absorbed in its heritage.

The building continued to reveal is myriad architectural secrets and rendered certain surprises that enriched their lives there.

And, what about those stories–that wild tangle of tales?

"Fantasy," she exclaimed.

What about George Roberts, the "fiend?"

"Well," she said, "there may have been a George Roberts somewhere, but not in our house." She recounted the procession of Roberts family members–and nary a George among them.

But, that fact does not diminish the Roberts House as a bona fide haunted house.

"The house was abandoned at the end of the 1800s," she continued, "and became derelict. It must have really looked like a haunted house."

She couldn't pinpoint the author or exact date, but she did recall what could have been the first reference to the haunting in the 1880s or '90s.

"It was the journal of a man who was coming along Old Gulph Road and was approaching our house. He wrote in his journal, 'I'm approaching the John Roberts House. It's haunted, they say.'"

What, then, was Christine Jones's reaction when she first heard that her beloved home was haunted?

"I think it's all very interesting," she said as she reeled off several odd and eerie incidents which played out in her and her husband's former home in Connecticut.

Ghosts are nothing new to Christine Jones.

"Actually, I'm sort of transfixed with them," she said. "I enjoy them. I try to see if I can connect.

"But, if John Roberts is connected to me, it's through other people who I call receptors."

Such individuals included the previous owners of the

home, who told the Joneses that on some occasions, certain items moved on their own inside the house.

"And just recently," Christine said, "when my husband was working on the historical society book, he contacted somebody who, when he found out where we lived, said that in the 1940s he had dated a girl who had lived in the house and one night when they were alone there, they heard footsteps in the house.

"I don't base much of anything on that. However, I do base some of the hauntings on this:

"We moved here in early 1983. We had roofers come in and they were going upstairs to the fourth level. The roofer went up first, and his helper, who was about 20 years old, followed him. I followed behind.

"We were part-way up a little curved stairway when the boy looked around with a real weird look on his face. I asked him what was the matter.

"He asked me if the house was haunted. I asked him why he asked. He said 'there's something I feel up here.' Whereupon, he started to tell me about other houses and other experiences he'd had."

In the winter of 1994, another "receptor" may have been brushed by whatever and whoever haunts the Roberts house. That individual was a heater repair man.

"He was down in the basement. Of course, I went down to snoop. He asked me if I had just opened a door or window upstairs. Now, he could not have felt anything down there even if I had. I said no.

"But, anyway, he said that an icy draft came in. It came around him. And then, it was as if someone put a cold, gentle hand on his shoulder.

"He said it wasn't like any draft he had ever felt before."

She later found out that he had also experienced several unearthly encounters in other homes. He, she reckoned, was a receptor.

Even as this book was being researched, more gaps in this story were at once being closed, and opened.

But, as the writer went to press, Christine Jones went home. To the Roberts House. The John Roberts III House. The Haunted House.

"Oh," she sighed with her typical ebullience, "I know that if there is a ghost, it almost has to be poor, unjustly hanged John. And, I know that he would not be a bad ghost–that he would be good."

The last remaining wall of the old Roberts Mill,
as seen in spring, 2000.

Graeme Park, the Keith House
The Governor's Daughter

As you approach the old Keith House, you may get the feeling that it shouldn't be there.

As you wander through the stark rooms of the place, you may get the feeling that *you* shouldn't be there–and that someone else might be there, just over your shoulder.

That someone else might very well be the forlorn spirit that inhabits the historic property.

The old, stone house stands in a park setting just a stone's throw from the sprawling Willow Grove Naval Air Station Joint Reserve Base and just around the bend from bustling Route 611.

The house, like the quiet land around it, is a survivor.

While it is indeed the Keith House, it is more commonly (and officially) known as Graeme Park. Or, to be historically accurate, it is "Fountain Low."

31

That aqueous name was derived from the presence of many springs on the property in 1722 when Sir William Keith commissioned construction of the mansion.

Keith was the provisional governor of Pennsylvania at the time, but shortly after his colonial home was completed, a rift with the Penn family resulted in his removal from that office. Keith eventually died penniless in the Old Baily Prison in London.

Keith's "plantation" was sold in 1739 to Dr. Thomas Graeme, a Philadelphia physician and Supreme Court judge.

Graeme used the quiet country estate as a summer retreat and remodeled it in the finest of English styles of the time. His social functions there became legendary.

The legend lived on after his death when his daughter, Elizabeth, continued the tradition.

Along with Elizabeth came a certain amount of intrigue and tragedy.

The well-educated Miss Graeme was a gracious hostess and circulated among the elite of Colonial Pennsylvania.

A romance with Benjamin Franklin's son, William, ended unhappily, and Elizabeth wound up marrying an undistinguished Scotsman named Henry Fergusson.

Fergusson was an avowed supporter of the British cause, and during the Revolution, Graeme Park was declared the property of a traitor and sold at auction. Fergusson (also referred to as Ferguson) fled to his homeland.

After the war, friends of Elizabeth Graeme Fergusson rallied and returned the property to her. Drained both physically and financially, however, Elizabeth was forced to sell the land in 1791.

Since then, the property has been owned by the Penrose and then the Strawbridge families, which both maintained the integrity of the land and its buildings with scrupulous attention.

Owned by the state since 1958, Graeme Park is remarkable in that it is the only surviving residence of a

Colonial Pennsylvania governor.

Alas, if the rustic walls of Gov. Keith's and Dr. Graeme's old home could talk, they would tell of the laughter and the lavish parties–the good times.

They would speak of the times that notables such as Gen. "Mad Anthony" Wayne and George Washington strategized and, yes, slept there. They would tell of the secret hiding places within the walls and floorboards of the mansion.

They would mourn, as well, for Elizabeth's miseries. For the failed dreams and unrequited love of a woman whose passions included the writing of romantic poetry.

And, those walls do echo with the sound of ghosts–at least one or two which could be considered to be among the "official ghosts" of Pennsylvania.

I say "official" because in the 1970s, the state's Bureau of Travel Development published a public information sheet which listed and located a dozen of Pennsylvania's most famous and accessible "haunted" sites.

On the top of the list was Graeme Park, which, according to the state bureau, is "haunted by the ghosts of Hugh and Elizabeth Ferguson who walk along the nearby pond in the moonlight."

Sketchy information, to be sure. But, over the years, the story of the Graeme Park hauntings has generated much interest and much ink.

In a 1958 feature story about the restoration of the Keith House, *The Daily Intelligencer* of Doylestown mentioned the ghosts of Henry and Elizabeth who, according to writer Rose Dewolf, "on moonlight night, can be seen sitting together in the crotch of the huge old tree behind the mansion."

In the *Intelligencer* a decade later, reporter Eric M. Boswell opened his feature story, "Some say that late at night the ghost of Elizabeth Ferguson roams through the large stone mansion and out across the lawns and wooded grounds of the once-sprawling colonial plantation."

"Previous tenants," he continued, "have been known to

knock softly on the door before entering the old house and murmur, 'Elizabeth, I'm coming in.'"

Other newspapers and magazines have added fuel to the phantasmic fire at Graeme Park, relating reports of Elizabeth Graeme's apparition near the big tree, along the pond, on a balcony of the house, or inside the house.

And, still another story tells of pilots reporting odd, glowing forms floating across the lawns of Graeme Park–a sort of ground-bound (and, excuse me here...) Unidentified Floating Objects.

A plane bound for Willow Grove soars over the Graeme Park barn.

❖

But let us now examine more contemporary sightings and sensings of the ghost of the governor's daughter.

For those, we visited with Patty Mousley, the Museum Educator at Graeme Park.

*The pond at Graeme Park figures in that historic site's
ghostly sightings.*

35

When Ms. Mousley assumed that position in the early 1990s, she was apprised by staff, visitors and volunteers of the tales about Elizabeth. She also rummaged through files of clippings about the legends that have been told about the property.

"I think the one I heard repeated the most was the one of people seeing the shapes or forms out by the pond," she said. That, of course, was reported by, among others, the pilots flying in and out of the nearby airfield.

"We've often wondered if it might have been a case of maybe the flags were up on the pole and maybe it was their reflections on the pond that looked like figures," she shrugged in an attempt to rationalize the sightings.

Mousley was referring to the American and Pennsylvania flags which do flutter on a pole adjacent to the pond. But, it seems hardly believable that their reflections on the water would have sparked such reports.

Again, she shrugged. "Who that is, or why they're here, we don't know."

She did recall some sketchy incidents that might be traced to Elizabeth's wandering spirit.

"In the time that I've been here," she said, "people have reported the smell of lilac in the house.

"One of the volunteers also told me she remembered leaving one of the rooms and hearing a sound going in the background—the sound of a spinning wheel spinning. And, there was nobody in the room!

"And, some of the volunteers have spoken about past holiday celebrations we have had where we decorate the house. Things had been placed nicely on window sills, and when they left and came back, those things would be on the floor, with no explanation."

And, not too long ago, a visitor told park employees that they had not only seen a mysterious, ghostly form lurking around the Visitor Center/barn on the property, but had taken a photograph which proved it.

But alas, "That picture's long since disappeared," Mousley lamented.

MONTGOMERY COUNTY GHOST STORIES

One of the most popular regular events at Graeme Park over the years has been a Halloween story-telling program.

"In it," Mousley said, "we tell the story of Elizabeth's dear dog Fidel. When Fidel died, she really did invite the whole community in for the burial service.

"Somewhere on the grounds, and nobody knows exactly where, she buried her beloved dog."

So, we asked her, does Fidel's canine spirit wander the grounds?

She arched her eyebrows, shrugged once more, and smiled coyly as if to say, "well, who knows??"

Patty Mousley is not fazed by the possibility or probability that she walks among the spirits at Graeme Park.

"Actually, no, because I feel that hopefully it would be people who lived here and they would see that we're carrying on the house and keeping their stories going and actually preserving their past. Hopefully, they would be happy with it."

The summer kitchen at Graeme Park.

37

Ruins along the Perkiomen, near the legendary "Ellinger's"

Headless Horsemen, Wheels of Fire, and Ghostly Dogs

When in pursuit of an area's legends and ghost stories, the road of research sometimes takes odd and unanticipated twists and turns.

Such is the case of several tales which have circulated around Schwenksville for more than a century.

38

MONTGOMERY COUNTY GHOST STORIES

They are tales of witches, murders, mysterious graves, skeletons, and ghosts of all ilk. And, they were collected and retold by a very respected, but unexpected individual.

A Pennsylvania governor.

But first, let us venture into the storied Goschenhoppen of northwestern Montgomery County.

Its undefined boundaries spread beyond the borders of Montgomery and into portions of Berks and Lehigh counties. It is the Upper Perkiomen region where the Pennsylvania Dutch Country rubs cultural shoulders with the Philadelphia suburbs.

"It is an 18th century folk region that was established in the folk mind prior to all the surveys. After all, at one time this was all Philadelphia County."

The words are those of pre-eminent folklorist and historian Donald F. ("Abe") Roan, a keeper of the folklore flame in Goschenhoppen.

"The people here ignored the political lines," he continued. "They couldn't, of course, for elections and taxes, but as far as farms and families, they lived in Goschenhoppen."

Speaking to the authors at the Goschenhoppen Library in Green Lane, Roan set the stage for this chapter. At the time, he did not know, however, what stories we would later uncover a little downstream along the Perkiomen Creek.

"Folk stories," he said, "will be found in patterns throughout regions. In the Pennsylvania Dutch Country, for example, you can find references to the Eewich Jaeger, or "Eternal Hunter," in Lancaster, Berks, and Schuylkill counties [Ed. Note: *See Pennsylvania Dutch Country Ghosts, Legends & Lore* or *Ghost Stories of Berks County*, by this author]—and the story, more or less, follows a pattern.

"And that's true of folk stories in most every culture throughout the world. The way they're told and the conditions happening in the stories are often similar, or relatively similar. It's part of an almost worldwide pattern."

That pattern is similar to the relatively recent phenomenon known as the "Urban Legend," in which certain stories circulate, literally, around the world–with several key elements the same no matter where the alleged "true" story took place.

Think of the "Eternal Hunter," then, as a "Rural Legend."

"It's the same with ghost stories," Roan added. "And, it's an interesting thing because there's an ancient Hebrew and an ancient Pennsylvania Dutch folk belief that says you can't get to heaven unless you have all your parts.

"In literature, Ichabod Crane was chased by the headless horseman and Washington Irving said the reason that fellow was eternally riding up and down the Hudson River Valley near Tarrytown is that he was a Revolutionary War soldier who had his head blown off by a cannonball. Now, he's looking for his head. He can't rest until he has all his parts. Now, that's a pretty common pattern."

Roan said there is even a legend of a Headless Horseman in the Schwenksville area.

"I picked this up when I moved into the area in 1964. Different people would tell me about a headless horseman who traveled up and down what is now Route 73 just east of Schwenksville.

"One neighbor told me that they were coming back from a lodge meeting, back in the days of the Model T Ford, and they passed the specter–the ghost–galloping in the other direction."

Others, Roan added, have also seen the headless ghost.

"Several other people there told me that they had been traveling along the road near the Pennypacker Mill and where the branch of the Perkiomen Creek comes in, and it's always in that location.

"So, he was apparently rather well-known in the area, at the time when people were entertaining each other around the cookstove or the fireplace, where those stories were told."

Let us now wander from the Upper Perkiomen region

MONTGOMERY COUNTY GHOST STORIES

south to Schwenksville.

Lurid tales of skulls buried in wells and evil innkeepers pepper the pages of history in the that section of the Perkiomen Valley.

Research by the Perkiomen Watershed Conservancy revealed the long-standing story of a Reading merchant bound for Philadelphia who was accosted and murdered by highwaymen on the old Perkiomen Road near Schwenksville–one possible baseline of the "headless horseman" legend.

A booklet published by the Schwenksville Bicentennial Committee in 1976 also mentioned the ghost of an old copper mine which operated from about 1720 to 1776 "in the vicinity of what is now the Mennonite Cemetery."

"Over the years," the article stated, "many strange tales of the mine were circulated, one of which involves two adventurers who were determined to find the hidden ore. They entered the shaft with candles and began working at removing some heavy stones that blocked their way. After the removal of several stones, an icy blast hit them and blew out the candles.

"They hastily withdrew, claiming that a 'spirit' of the mine guarded the treasure."

Another account in the files of the county Historical Society confirmed that there was such a copper mine in that area, and it actually dated to as early as 1695.

But, to ratchet-up our efforts to present Montgomery County's most enduring legends to another generation, we visited the archives of Pennypacker Mills, Schwenksville.

The staff at the county historical site was kind enough to ferret out a series of documents in the handwriting of none other than Pennsylvania Governor Samuel W. Pennypacker.

Pennypacker Mills stands like an English Manor House on 15 acres of countryside near the Perkiomen Creek. A "Country Gentleman's Estate," its conservators call it.

In a curious coincidence of succession, the land upon which the mansion is situated was deeded, over time, by a

41

Modern housing encroaches on the forlorn monument that marks the anonymous graves of Revolutionary War soldiers near Pennypacker Mills.

42

Penn (William) to a Pennington (William) to a Pennypacker (Peter).

But perhaps its most illustrious resident was Samuel Pennypacker, who took possession in 1900 and enlarged it to its present dimensions.

A native of Phoenixville who set up a legal practice in Philadelphia, Pennypacker served in the state capital from 1903 to 1907 and then returned to his estate, where he died in 1916.

The mansion is noteworthy not only for its gubernatorial connections, but also for the fact that (and pardon me for this) *George Washington Slept There.*

It was late September and early October, 1777, before and after the American defeat at the Battle of Germantown, that the general and his troops camped at the abandoned mill.

That bivouac at Pennypacker's has generated its own intrigue over the centuries. Rumors of unmarked graves of soldiers were prevalent, as were various superstitions attached to the mounds of soil which supposedly covered the burials.

On occasion, tangles of human bones emerged from that ground during storm runoffs or field plowing.

This was a backwater area then, a fair distance from any sizable settlement, and traditions died hard along the Perkiomen.

In his intense and extensive conversations with locals, Governor Pennypacker recorded numerous recollections of witches, hexerei and bizarre beliefs.

In 1907, Gov. Pennypacker wrote after talking with Mrs. William D. Hunsicker, "Belief in witches is common." And, the 78 year old "Mammy" Keller later said, "Some people thought old Mrs. G— was a witch. Henry Satz' wife had a baby. He likewise had a vendue and Mrs. G— went there and offered to hold the baby in her lap. 'Do not let her touch it,' said a horrified neighbor woman. 'She is a witch!'"

What's more, a Dr. Bechtel elaborated on Mrs. G— and

43

MONTGOMERY COUNTY GHOST STORIES

her alleged sorcery, and named other local women who were believed to be witches.

"Daniel Pennypacker," Dr. Bechtel told Gov. Pennypacker of his ancestor, "firmly believed in witches and over his doorway were found many pins driven in to kill the witches.

"Mrs. Puhl, Isaac Puhl's mother, used to pow-wow—words were used to stop bleeding. If wounded, the ax or implement must not be permitted to rust. A stake turned around in the fence would stop a cross dog from biting and barking. To spit on the under side of a stone and turn it down would stop a pain in the side."

This type of faith healing, this pow-wowing, was yet another Pennsylvania German custom that was quite common up to the early years of the 20th century in the "Dutch Country."

But, the most chilling stories from Gov. Pennypacker's files are those of a legendary family of alleged ne'er-do-wells named Ellinger.

According to the aforementioned "Mammy" Keller, "The Ellingers were the old man, the old woman, four boys and a girl."

In a conversation on February 26, 1907, the 78-year old woman told the governor, "The old man was large and stout, grim and sinister."

Five years earlier, W.D. Hunsicker told Gov. Pennypacker that the Ellingers were originally blacksmiths. "A very bad lot. The whole neighborhood feared them. The house was a large, two and one-half story stone, and a stone barn."

And, if the recollections of others were correct, the Ellingers also operated a tavern, in which they sold the product of their illicit still. Dr. Bechtel even claimed that "Mrs. E. would persuade the peddlers to her embraces and then at a certain signal Ellinger came and robbed them."

"On the place adjoining Pennypacker's Mill to the eastward just beyond the stone bridge over the branch along the Skippack Road stood an old tavern," Rev. Hunsicker

44

said. "It belonged to a family of bad reputation called Ellinger.

"Travellers who sought its shelter disappeared and were heard of no more. Once, a drover going to the west to buy cattle rode upon horseback to this ill-fated inn. He and his horse were thrown into the well and the well was then filled up."

The reputed dastardly deeds of the Ellingers sparked the ghost stories which were sure to follow.

"After their time," Rev. Hunsicker continued, "the house was haunted by spooks. At night, lights could be seen about it and white horses without heads wandered around it. About the grounds were places where the snow would not lie in the winter, disclosing the graves of those who had been murdered for their money."

Gov. Pennypacker noted that another neighbor had told him the name of the drover who was thrown into the well with his horse was named Reuben Boorse, of Kulpsville.

"He was last seen at Skippack riding a white horse," the story continued. "And, a headless rider on a white horse still appears around the remains of the old tavern."

The headless rider was certainly not the only manifestation of the ghosts there.

"Once," the governor wrote, "Jesse Grimly was passing the house. Suddenly a rolling ball of fire came running down the hill. He plunged into the Perkiomen and was nearly drowned!"

The roster of horrifying events at the old Ellinger place is testimony to the terror felt by those in the Schwenksville area as they remembered the evil events and their aftermath.

August 9, 1903:
Hardman tells me that one night about fifteen years ago, Charles H. Tube, a young man, and an undertaker living near Skippack came to Schwenksville to attend a Society meeting. After it was over he and his wife drove home. When they reached Ellingers a calf came out from the Ellinger ruins and

45

approached the carriage.

Both saw it distinctly—in astonishment and fear they discovered that it was without a head. It clung close to the wagon until they drove hurriedly away.

September 4, 1903:

About six years ago, Henry Wireman, who lived on the high ground upon the opposite side of the branch from me was going up the hill at night by a path from the Ellinger ruins on his way home. He was chased by a phantom with eyes as large as plates.

July 8, 1905; Told to me by Frank Schwenk:

About fifteen years ago Frank Ziegler of Lederachsville was riding about 11 o'clock at night past the Ellinger place upon his black horse. The horse suddenly stopped, trembled in every muscle, and refused to move. What appeared to be a huge, white dog came out from the ruins into the road and then, melting into shadow, disappeared.

On one occasion, Frank Wireman, while riding by the place at night, saw coming toward him a man driving a cow and a calf. There was nothing strange about the fact save that it happened at night. But when they approached, behold, they were all skeletons! And looking between their bones he could see the objects beyond by the uncertain light of the moon. He whipped up his horse and hastened away from the unhallowed surroundings.

September, 1907:

Mr. Henry Landis, an assistant principal of one of the Philadelphia public schools, tells me that he was born on a farm along the branch near Schwenksville and that in his youth he heard this story: A man and his wife were driving at night along the Skippack Road in front of the Ellinger ruins. The horse stopped and trembled. A huge white dog came out, reared upon his hind legs, and with wide-open jaws, thrust his head forward into the wagon as if to seize them. The man, frightened at the unearthly spectacle, whipped up his horse. They then looked back, saw the specter still standing upreared when it suddenly faded into mist and, without movement, disappeared.

Gov. Samuel Pennypacker was a seminarian, a teacher,

a lawyer, a judge, a Civil War veteran, and an historian. A former president of the Historical Society of Pennsylvania, the "gentleman farmer" left as his legacy dozens of books and papers written by him, thousands of books accumulated by him–and a fascinating pack of important, old-fashioned ghost stories collected by him.

The Jarrettown Hotel.

The "Lady in White"

I waited in the corridor of the Jarrettown Hotel anticipating my meeting with the proprietor of the Upper Dublin Township landmark.

As I sat on an ancient bootblack stand manufactured by "Gaetano Seccia, 13th St., Phila.," surrounded by antiques and faux antiques, classic paintings and vintage maps, I got a feel for the pride that proprietor has in his old inn.

I was to meet first, however, with the manager of the hotel–a soft-spoken gentleman who preferred to remain nameless in this story. In exchange for his account of the ghosts of the hotel, I deferred to his wishes.

48

MONTGOMERY COUNTY GHOST STORIES

We sat in his cozy third-floor garret office as he spoke of his unsettling experiences there.

"I was up here by myself at night–which, by the way, will never happen again," he began.

I chuckled at that declaration. He did not. And as the mood of the conversation sobered, he continued his hair-raising story.

"The water started running in the bathroom," he said. "I got up and turned the water off. I looked around. There was nobody else up here.

"I came and sat down in my office and the water started running at the other end of the hall, in another bathroom."

He looked around again, and he was still alone.

Or was he?

"I sat back down again, and both toilets flushed on their own!

"I had been counting money up here. I left the money on the desk, left the building, and I will never come back up here again at night!"

That night, the manager had no reason to suspect any untoward events. But, he had witnessed other events, at other times, with others around him in other parts of the hotel.

There was the time that he and four other employees were sitting in the first-floor corridor that splits the dining room and the bar. It was about 2:30 in the morning. The restaurant had closed, and they were the only ones still there.

They were distracted by a light that flickered on the main staircase. The manager went up the steps and switched the light off.

As he walked away, the light switched itself back on.

"And," he continued, "all five of us tried to get out the back door at the same time!"

He recalled a similar incident. "There was a lamp on a table downstairs, and every time Joe walked in the room, it went on-off-on-off. When he walked out of the room, it went off-on-off-on."

Present at the time of that incident was a handyman customer who witnessed the oddity. He took the lamp apart, checked its wiring and connections, shook it, put it back together, checked the plug–even spread the prongs on the plug to make sure it was seated snugly in the socket.

All seemed to be tight and tidy–until Joe came back into the room. "When," the manager said, "the light went off-on-off again!"

"Joe" is Guiseppe Randazzo, the proprietor of the inn and one who embraces the energies–the ghosts–which call the ca. 1847 hotel their eternal home.

Guiseppe's experiences with those energies go far beyond simple power and plumbing glitches. Deeply spiritual and cognizant of the realm of the supernatural, the affable entrepreneur spoke through a lilting Sicilian accent and offered addenda to his manager's recollections.

Guiseppe introduced us to a veritable cast of ghostly characters who, in turn, add another kind of character to the historic building. He and his manager spoke first of...The Lady in White.

"We were interviewing a girl for a job," Guiseppe said. "There was a woman surveyor outside who came in and asked us who the pretty lady up at the second floor window was.

"She described the woman in the window as having a pretty face, red hair, and a white dress."

Of course, there was no one, no lady in a white dress, at that window, in that room, or even anywhere upstairs.

But, from time to time, there is a spirit on the second floor–one who has been known to torment women who use the rest room there.

"We had a customer," Joe said, "who went into the ladies room and was approached by a young girl who said, 'Don't worry, I'm not going to hurt you.'

"That woman didn't even finish what she went to the ladies room to do. She came downstairs to tell us about it when she noticed a picture we have hanging on a wall and

50

she shouted, 'That's the girl!'"

The female ghost, or ghosts, on the second floor is not alone in the Jarrettown Hotel. A medium who was brought in to entertain patrons also "read" the building and identified several spirits.

"She said she detected two male spirits in the bar area," Joe said, "and a lady on the landing of the stairs up to the third floor."

Joe said he is sensitive to the energies that swirl in the hotel. "I feel it. There's an electricity–a tingling. But, it doesn't bother me."

A former employee reported witnessing the figure of a man washing his hands in a sink in a third floor room which has been converted into an office–a sink which still stands but was long ago disconnected from its plumbing.

What's more, both employees and customers say they have detected activity in such gloomy places as the inn's basement and a closed-off staircase.

"A while ago," Joe said, "a manager was on his way out, and we always check the basement door before we leave. Well, the door was opened, so he went down to check. By the time he got downstairs into the basement, he heard several loud footsteps–*boom, boom, boom*. He came back up. He knew he was alone, but he started yelling everybody's name–'Joe, Dave...anybody? Anybody here? Talk to me!' There was nobody else there."

If that basement, if those walls of the hotel could talk, they would have many stories of human drama to tell. Among the most tragic incidents took place on May 28, 1896, when a tornado ripped through Jarrettown. At the hotel, two men were killed when a stable wall collapsed on them.

As we sat in that third floor office, others–a neighbor, an assistant manager–joined us. Each expanded the dimensions of the stories of the Jarrettown haunting.

Assistant manager Pat McGee reported seeing flickering lights and shadowy figures lurking behind illuminated windows in the empty building long after closing time.

51

MONTGOMERY COUNTY GHOST STORIES

"We have one incident," Joe recalled, "that happens almost every week."

As those in the room nodded their heads in agreement, he elaborated. "If we're here after 2:30 in the morning, somebody will try to tell us to get out."

And, Joe said, that "somebody's" urgings can be quite effective.

"Glasses will start falling from the bar. They could fall one on top of another, but they will never break. That really has happened, and happened often."

Joe remembered another incident when a framed antique map seemingly "flew" from its hanging on a third floor wall long after closing time–perhaps another spectral message for those still there to go home.

Joe truly believes it is the spirit of the Lady in White, seeking solace and silence for the night.

"She's actually walking around here, we believe, and she wants to rest. She wants everybody out!"

We wandered through the warren of rooms on the second floor, to the sealed staircase and into dark and foreboding spaces. Joe reaffirmed his feelings about his haunted hotel.

"I have no problems with it. And, lots more than what I've told you has happened. I could go on for days with the stories."

There have never been any violent episodes, never anything more than gentle words, the fleeting glimpse of a beautiful woman, or the occasional burst of poltergeist-like activity.

"They don't do any harm" Joe said. "I've had people who told me how I could get rid of them, but I'd never want to."

Joe, whose contact with the "other side" has extended beyond the walls of the Jarrettown Hotel and into his home, has a refreshing–and quite glib–way of summing up his thoughts about his resident wraiths: "They're neat," he said with a gleam in his eyes.

"That's all I can say, they're neat."

Several people say the "Lady in White" wanders this and other rooms at the Jarrettown Hotel.

The Phantom of Fifth Street

"If ever a house was haunted, this is it!!"

They are the words of a Pottstown couple whose names are being withheld at their request.

Also kept anonymous is the exact address of the house they moved into in September, 1986.

Suffice to say that it is somewhere among the duplexes, singles, and rowhomes of Fifth Street in the borough.

And, it is haunted by a spirit the couple–let us call them Jim and Gerri–call "Pete."

The previous owners of the home were two elderly women who grew up within its walls. They had moved to Florida, supposedly to put some distance between them and that house.

In a series of e-mails from Jim and Gerri, their harrowing experiences unfolded dramatically.

"When we first moved into the house, it was in need of much repair. Not long after we moved in we had a problem with blinking lights and fading electricity. The wiring was checked out by an electrician and the electric company inspected the outside wiring. No problems were found.

"And there were the footsteps we heard at all hours of the night, up and down the stairs, in the hallway, and up in the attic. No reason was found for any of the noise. Our oldest daughter was afraid to sleep in her room. Most mornings we woke up to find her sleeping outside our bedroom door. She told us she heard the door knob to the attic rattling, and also heard the footsteps. At first we thought she just had an overactive imagination, but then we started experiencing the unexplained."

Keys, mail, kitchen items were lost–and then found in the most unlikely places. At first, the couple blamed one another. But, after a while the explanations and the accusations made no sense.

Answers to some of those questions eventually came–

54

from a most surprising source.

About a year after they moved in, they said, the two women who had lived there before them came to call. And, they shared a strange story with Jim and Gerri.

"They told us they moved away because they were afraid of their mother. They said after she died, she never left the house. "Their fear was evident when they refused to come in and see all the changes we made to the house."

The women told them that their mother "practiced the old ways." They said their mother spent much time alone in the attic. It was her room.

And, perhaps, it still is. Perhaps her ghost still rambles in that house on Fifth Street.

"One day we came home from the grocery store," Gerri said, "and as I was putting groceries away in the kitchen cabinets, I saw a large, dark shadow go by me and walk into the dining room. A minute later, Jim came into the kitchen and wanted me to guess who he just saw. Of course, I got it right. After she walked by me, she went into the dining room then into the hallway to the front door to Jim. We saw the dark figure all the time. Sometimes we would feel the cold air and then we would feel the presence or see the dark figure."

The "dark figure" continued to come in and out of their lives as long as they resided in the house.

"My husband saw her one stormy night," Gerri continued. "We had both fallen asleep downstairs, I on the sofa and he on a chair. John awoke and saw her standing in the kitchen. She was wearing a blue dress or bathrobe. John looked at me to make sure it wasn't me in the other room. When he looked back, the figure was gone.

"He never told me that night–he knew if he did, I would not have slept the rest of the night!"

Jim concurred. "When I saw her that night, she didn't appear as a shadow. She looked solid. I couldn't see her face but I could tell she was wearing blue. The really strange thing was that when I saw her it was like I could feel her sadness. It was overwhelming."

"The noises in the house scared my wife so badly that she wouldn't sleep upstairs without me," he added. "She would wake up at four in the morning to make a new bed on the sofa when I left for work."

Jim also confirmed that he and Gerri had often heard footsteps. "Many nights Gerri would wake me up to listen to the sound of someone walking down the hall toward the bathroom and up the attic stairs. We could hear it so clear that we knew she shuffled her feet."

Still more of Jim and Gerri's questions may have been answered when they received a phone call from Florida. It was one of the old woman's daughters.

"She told me that her mother wore a blue house coat all the time...and dragged her feet when she walked," Jim noted.

As time went by, Jim, Gerri, and the ghost settled into an uneasy relationship. "It seems that she got used to 'living' with us and we got used to 'living' with her," Gerri said.

But when the couple learned that they would be moving from the house, it could well be that their ghostly companion found out, too–and was not happy about it.

"All hell broke loose," said Gerri. "Things went bump in the night, all night! It sounded like furniture was being moved (and dropped) up in the attic. Jim refused to go check it out until morning. Nothing was amiss. This activity continued until we moved out."

Is the spirit still in that house? Does the "dark shadow" still glide throughout the dwelling? Jim is uncertain.

"I believe she may have tried to follow us after we moved. I told her to go home," he said. "I hope she has found her peace."

MONTGOMERY COUNTY GHOST STORIES

Things That Go *Slap* in the Night

Again, we change the names and generalize the location in this story from a Souderton woman who, along with her husband, were tormented by a demonstrative poltergeist in the Cape Cod-style home they moved into in 1983.

It had been previously occupied by a family whose patriarch had been sent to an institution as punishment for domestic offenses.

We shall call him "Mr. Smith."

"Mr. Smith" died in the institution about seven years before his wife passed, and the tellers of this tale moved in shortly after her death.

The current occupants said their unnerving experiences started just weeks after they moved in.

"My husband and I were sitting in the living room watching TV when we heard a very distinct *'slap-slap-slap'* on the wooden steps.

"We both looked at each other and really didn't know what to make of it. The steps were right in front of us and nobody was near them to make such a sound.

"This started to happen more often, and only in the evening at about 8 o'clock."

The couple purchased the home with the full knowledge of the troubles that once brewed within its walls.

"So," the woman said, "one night my husband jokingly went to the bottom of the steps and said, 'OK, Mr. Smith!'

"The *'slap-slap-slap'* seemed to answer him back!"

Whatever the meaning or significance of that was enough to further rattle the nerves of the homeowners.

"By now," the woman added, "this whole step thing was really becoming creepy to the point that I wouldn't stay home alone at night.

"We spoke to our pastor about it and he did not discount the possibility of some spiritual being. At the time, our church was having an addition built and our

57

pastor spoke to the foreman about our steps. He indicated that from a building perspective there was nothing that would physically cause the steps to make that kind of sound on their own."

They learned to live with the occasional "slapping" sound, and about eight months after they moved in they hired a contractor to build a full dormer on the third floor.

"That required that the old roof be torn off and the area redesigned. And since then, we have not had any step incidents and continue to live in the house with our son and dog."

But, there are still some unanswered questions that will linger forever with the family.

"Could there have been an unsettled spirit remaining in the house when we moved in? Did removing the roof release it or let it escape from the violence that took place in the house?

"Who knows?" she concluded. "And, quite frankly, I don't want to know!"

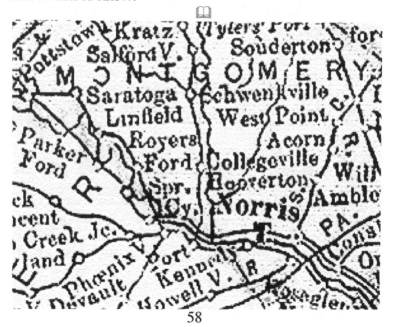

MONTGOMERY COUNTY GHOST STORIES

The Night Walker

Our next personal ghost story from a private home in Montgomery County comes from the Evansburg area. Again, we will omit the name of its teller to protect her family and their property.

The home on that land in Skippack Township was fairly new when her parents purchased it. Only one other family had previously resided there.

The woman's childhood memories of the place, where her mother still resided when she related her story, were pleasant...all things considered.

"Occasionally, I would see someone walking by the window—you'd look out and see flashes of color go by. There would be the sound of cars pulling into the driveway. I'd hear the car door slam, but there would be no car, and no people there.

"So, we'd have these weird noises."

But, the eeriest events took place inside the home, at one particular place, and usually at night. They were witnessed by several family members, and even a visitor.

"My brother and I had several experiences," she continued. "One night I woke up in the middle of the night. My brother's bedroom door was always kept closed. But this time, the door was open, and there was someone at the end of my brother's bed.

"I thought it was my mother. It was doing some sort of motions, like bending over and reaching over its head.

"All I could see was a dark figure. I really just assumed it was my mother. Then, it stopped its motion, started walking toward the window, and disappeared.

"Well, the next day I asked my mother about it, and she thought I was crazy. It wasn't her. She thought I must have been dreaming."

Could it have been that simple? Could the nocturnal manifestation been the product of her sleepy fantasy?

"Well, a couple days later my brother came to my mother with the same question. He wanted to know what she had been doing in his room, at the end of his bed, in the middle of the night.

"When he found out it wasn't her, he started sleeping with a baseball bat!"

An older sister also told tales of trembling glasses in cupboards, slamming doors, and a hand-mirror that floated in thin air and fell to the floor. She swore it wasn't childhood hysteria or an overactive imagination.

"There was nothing imaginative about this," she insisted. "In fact, we'd have people come over to the house and experience things. People would say they felt things brushing up against their legs, and some people said they'd see someone walking by, when there was nobody else in the house."

The woman was, and is certain that a ghost walked among them in their otherwise tranquil family home.

"The path he seems to travel is from the bathroom, across a short hallway to my brother's room–and gone." One time, her mother's friend from England paid a visit. She had no knowledge about the notion of a ghost in the house.

"She told us she was walking up the stairs and she passed who she thought was my father in the hallway. She said it was a man wearing a long coat.

"He said 'hello' to her. She said 'hello' back. And, when she came downstairs she told my mother that she just saw my father upstairs. My mom told her that she couldn't have–because he was at work.

"She said, well, somebody was upstairs. My mother said no, there was not!

"And then, my mother proceeded to tell her about our ghost."

No doubt, it was a story the British visitor never expected to hear from her host...and will never forget.

📖

Noises in Niantic

I turned off Route 100 into what could almost be considered the "Highlands" of Montgomery County.

I followed Niantic Road, weaving around and over the West Branch of the Perkiomen, into and through the crossroads village of Niantic, to the rustic farm of Sandra and William Lowery.

He is a blacksmith, she an artist. Both display their work at various venues, including the Goschenhoppen Folk Festival.

We sat in their living room, warmed on a midwinter morning by one of the woodburning stoves that provide all the heat the 200-year old farmhouse requires.

Here, on the very edge of the county, a far cry from the tangle of highways and waffled street patterns to the county's extreme eastern end, life is quieter, simpler. Although scattered clusters of new homes dot the landscape, this is Montgomery County almost untouched by the rampant growth to the south and east.

The Lowerys, unlike others, had no qualms about allowing their real names to be used in their story.

In tune with the land, its history, each other, and the compact farmhouse they've called home for more than 35 years, the two are quite frank about their individual approaches to the supernatural.

Bill Lowery spoke first. "We were only in this house a few years. We were all out in the car, but I had to come back into the kitchen to get something I had forgotten. I came in through the kitchen door, looked up across the kitchen and there was somebody looking out the front door.

"I opened up the kitchen door, and I must have blinked or something, but he was gone."

The distance between the door at the front of the home and the kitchen door is about 15 feet, and William couldn't reckon then or now how whoever had been standing there could have vanished, literally, in the blink of an eye.

"All right, maybe I just saw something like a shadow, or who knows?"

Bill maintained that he is still a "non-believer."

But–and it is a *big* but–he says there are many questions no one seems able to answer.

"I can't explain them," he admitted.

He can't explain who he hears calling his name from time to time while he is working or relaxing in the house or barn.

"I just hear it," he said. *"Bill...Bill.* Someone calls out my name, and there's nobody there."

With that, his wife picked up the conversation.

"We both started to pay closer attention after those things happened to him," Sandy said.

"I always want to find a logical reason for things, but little things kept happening. Then, I had a couple really good ones that still give me the chills."

Sitting where we were, directly under what had been the couple's daughter's bedroom, Sandra spoke of an incident that occurred there.

"It was the middle of the day, nobody was in the house," she recalled. "And all of a sudden, I heard something that was between a moan and a cry–and it was loud! It came from up there."

Sandy said she got up and went out the door in a flash. "This was so vivid. And what it was, I haven't a clue."

Sandra adamantly discounted any sounds of nature, a screaming cat, or any other logical source of the sound.

The couple reeled off several other strange things they've experienced on their otherwise comfortable farm. They remembered odd aromas–fresh paint, cinnamon, and others–that wafted through the house with no apparent source.

And, they tried to establish possible baselines of any hauntings there.

There are murmurings–the muffled sounds of conversation within the walls of the house. "You can't make out the words," Sandy said, "but we both have heard it."

"We were told," she continued, "that a little girl died in our attic. There was an old steamer trunk up there and apparently she climbed into it and the lid closed on her. I guess her parents couldn't find her and never thought of looking in the trunk. Well, she suffocated inside it."

Only their grown daughter, who once or twice felt a gentle touch on her shoulders while on the attic stairs, has any experiences which may be directly related to that little girl's death.

But, the most fascinating story attached to the house actually extends beyond the Lowerys' property and straddles the county line–down an old millrace and over the hills into the Berks County town of Bally.

"There was a fellow who lived in this house, sometime around the second world war, who would go over to the Bally Hotel fairly regularly.

"Well, one night, we've been told, he rented a room there and, for whatever reason, hanged himself in that room.

"Now, there's the belief that his ghost walks between the old hotel and this house."

Sandy admitted that sightings of the strolling ghost have been few and far between. But, the artist in her paints a haunting word picture.

"You can see him, in your mind's eye, gliding along that raceway by the old mill. It's a nice, lonely, dreary-looking place–an ideal place for a ghost."

Maybe, someday, that artist in her will render that gloomy vision on canvas. Until then, the wandering spirit– and the strange sights, smells, and sounds in their farmhouse and on their farm will exist only as enigmas.

📖

The Ghostly Indian
of the Evansburg Inn

"When a building has existed for almost two centuries it quite frequently picks up a ghost or two."

Such are the words in a paragraph on the menu of the Evansburg Inn.

Retaining its rustic, knotty-pine character, the inn at 3835 Germantown Pike dates to about 1767 when it was built as a farmhouse.

In 1801, the earliest of a procession of innkeepers set up shop in the building, and since then the handsome structure has served as everything from a stage coach stop to a highly-regarded country restaurant.

Suzanne and Joe Maslanka purchased the Evansburg Inn and have taken great pride in both the business and the building.

Just after the Maslankas took over, they asked a respected "sensitive" to "read" the place.

"She proceeded to tell us," Sue said, "that everyone who had this place before us ended up in divorce."

That alarming (and unsubstantiated) statement took Sue by surprise, until the reader continued. "She said, though, that we would not. She said we would be here for a very long time and make a lot of changes."

That "reading," incidentally, was made in 1972–and Sue and Joe have enjoyed both their professional and matrimonial lives together ever since.

"And," Sue continued, "she told us yes, we have spirits in here."

Sue said that as the medium absorbed the more than two centuries of history in the inn, she made some interesting claims.

"She insisted during a trance that she saw the figure of an Indian in full feathered regalia," Suzanne wrote in a statement about the inn's usually invisible occupants.

64

"She also claimed there was a room in the attic of the inn that was inhabited by the sad spirit of a wounded prisoner of war who died of his wounds before being freed."

According to Sue, the medium did not know until she was told that the inn was built on an Indian burial ground and had been used as a military hospital at one time.

Joe Maslanka said he is uncomfortable in some rooms upstairs, and others who have entered the lair of the sorrowful soldier's ghost upstairs say they have felt its presence.

The woman did assure the couple that they would have no troubles with the benign tenants—that they were happy with the changes that have been made in the place they call their eternal home.

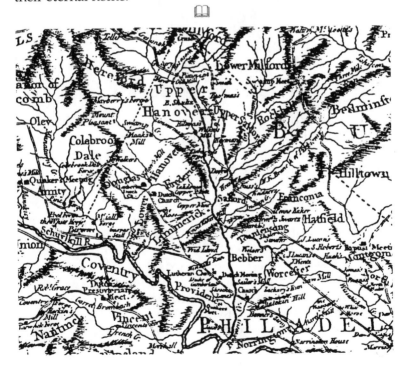

The "Presence"
at the General Lafayette Inn

If the proprietors of a rustic restaurant on the Germantown Pike in Lafayette Hill, Whitemarsh Township, were to be scrupulously correct, they would have named their historic place the General *Marie Joseph Paul Yves Roche Gilbert du Motier, Marquis de* Lafayette Inn.

But, they did not. Mercifully, they called it the General Lafayette Inn. In the 1950s, it was the Lafayette Hotel and long before that it went by the name of the Barren Hill Hotel, and The Three Tuns.

It's a wonder the restaurant exists at all. In 1958, the then-200 year old building had a date with the wrecking ball to make room for a gas station.

Former innkeeper Ludwig Zackiewicz is credited with sparing the building from that ignominious fate. And through a succession of later owners, the hotel struggled for a share of the area dining dollars and an identity.

With Mike McGlynn and his partners, who took possession in 1996, it found both.

Although few stretches of "Barren Hill" are devoid of development, there was a time when that crest on the very edge of Montgomery County was a remote but strategic ridge.

On May 20, 1778, a fierce skirmish between troops under Gen. Lafayette's command and a band of British soldiers erupted not far from the present restaurant.

Its role as witness to history is secure, and its reputation as a fine restaurant, B&B and microbrewery was building as this book was being compiled.

And, of course, the ca. 1752 building has some quirks about it–some of which have made Mike McGlynn and others believe they are never really alone there.

One former employee reported hearing footsteps plodding across the second floor. When he went upstairs to check on just who might be walking in what he knew was an empty room at the time, he found no one. The phenomenon repeated itself often.

Still another ex-employee claimed he saw a chair in the pool room spinning on one leg–a sight which left him frozen in amazement and questioning his own sanity.

As we toured the ancient inn which has hosted generals, the genteel, and the general public since before the Revolution, Mike McGlynn pointed out the architectural singularities and peculiarities of the building.

A restoration specialist by trade, McGlynn pointed out remnants of old staircases and evidence of its Colonial-era construction.

We crawled into the attic, where crossbeams still bear marks of Roman numerals carved in by early carpenters, and we looked at the building from the inside out.

Our tour eventually led to and beyond a saloon-style swinging door that separates the second-floor dining room from a corridor which leads to the McGlynn's office.

We walked down that corridor and stood before the office door, where the soft-spoken innkeeper spoke of the first of his brushes with whatever entities might roam the General Lafayette Inn.

"I was here about 3:30 in the morning," McGlynn said. "I was closing up for the night.

"I was getting ready to lock the door and I felt this presence behind me.

"My hair stood on end. I just sensed that there was a presence behind me.

"I was deathly afraid to turn around and face whatever it was. So, I immediately locked the door, took two steps walking, and then quickly ran out of the building!"

McGlynn's hasty escape was down a hallway which led laterally from where was standing, then down a back staircase, and out.

"It was one of those things. I can't point to any evidence. It's just that there was this very powerful presence behind me," he continued as he tried to reckon with the experience.

"I've had other things happen," he added, "mostly in the oldest part of the building."

There were several times that he would be sitting alone in the office and the knob on his office door twitched, twisted, and turned.

"Other people have heard that, too," he declared. "The knob rattles, as if somebody's trying to get in. Many a time I would get over, open the door really quickly, and there would be no one there."

That doorknob is one of the oldest, and perhaps original pieces of hardware in the building.

The General Lafayette Inn swirls with rumors of soldiers who were brought there and may have died there. And, there are those who say the ghosts of those soldiers may be the cause of the perceived "presences" in the building.

Does that prospect bother Mike McGlynn?

"Oh no," he shrugged. "I'm not afraid of them. Maybe it's the fact that I identify so much with the building–that

I've worked on every part of the building during the restoration.

"Maybe the ghosts are comfortable with me—and my presence!"

The "haunted hallway" of the General Lafayette Inn.

69

Researcher David J. Seibold walking the edge of Ringing Rocks.

The Legend of Ringing Rocks

Throughout eastern Pennsylvania are geological anomalies that have given rise over the centuries to legends linking them to the very root of all evil and the unknown.

Near Easton in Northampton County is Hexenkopf, an outcrop of rocks where, tradition has it, witches cavort and spirits spiral.

MONTGOMERY COUNTY GHOST STORIES

On the Blue Mountain ridge in Berks, Lehigh, and Schuylkill counties are several natural wonders where giant boulders are strewn for acres across the hillsides.

The largest of these fields of stone is the "Blue Rocks" of northeastern Berks, which extends nearly a mile on the slope of the mountain. The Blue Rocks Felsenmeere, or "rock sea" is considered to be the largest of its kind in Pennsylvania.

Whether strewn by glacier or other ancient natural effect, the Blue Rocks are the setting for an enduring folk tale. Early settlers heard stories from the natives of a fiery dragon which leaped from Dragon Cave, several miles to the south, and onto or near the Blue Rocks. The dragon represented the restless spirits of a pair of Indian lovers who died in a suicide pact in the cave.

Another superstition has it that the Blue Rocks and other Felsenmeere on the mountain ridge and beyond were the work of a clumsy Satan.

In his 1925 *Reading and Berks County: A History*, Cyrus T. Fox said, "Numerous theories have been offered to account for the origin of such boulder fields.

"One of these explanations, current among unlettered folk and children, is that stones grew from stone seed.

"The stones in the soil and the rocks in the fields, both hindrances to the farmers and their work, have grown from stone seeds sowed by the Devil. In some places, as upon mountain sides and in localities such as the 'Blue Rocks' and 'Ringing Rocks' near Pottstown, the string of the bag in which he carried his rock seed broke or became loose and a greater quantity of seed came out of the bag than elsewhere. So, as to such a place, these folks say, 'Here the Devil's bag string broke.'"

Such rock-strewn fields surrounding the Unami and Ridge Valley creeks near Sumneytown have been called "The Devil's Potato Patch."

Which brings us to Ringing Rocks, in Lower Pottsgrove Township.

Not to be confused with the Bucks County park of the

same name (and where, some say, paranormal events have and are taking place), Montgomery County's Ringing Rocks is a 37-acre recreation area acquired by the township in 1998.

Before that, the trolley line from Pottstown carried townsfolk to what was a bucolic summer retreat complete with a hotel, cabins and homes, a pond, a roller rink, and pleasant picnic groves and trails.

Immensely popular with Pottstonians in the second half of the 19th century, the attraction even inspired a music work by B. Frank Walters, "Sounds From the Blue Rocks: A Romantic Fantasy," in 1864.

More than that, Ringing Rocks inspired a powerful legend which is worth repeating in this volume.

Throughout the years, writers have waxed eloquently on the cause and effect of Ringing Rocks and the facts and fables attached to them.

Most eloquent of those publications could well be have been an unattributed "History of Ringing Rocks Park" found in a file in the Pottstown Public Library.

Its author made a rather grandiose claim when he or she called the Ringing Rocks "the greatest natural phenomenon between the Delaware and Ohio rivers."

That bold boast aside, the writer asserted that "A halo of romance environs the spot, and the departing footsteps of its Indian possessors are marked in legend everywhere."

Before we proceed any further, let us account for the name, Ringing Rocks. Basically, the Lower Pottsgrove boulders and their Bucks County cousins give off, at best, a clunky resonance when struck by a hammer or hard object.

But, that reality did not dismay the early observer who claimed that beyond their mundane melodiousness, the Ringing Rocks have "the power to make the music of one of Handel's oratorios or awaken the sweetest melodies that ever lingered in the brains of Mozart or Mendelssohn. All the notes of the scale can be rung from this mysterious music box of Dame Nature."

This hyperbolic writer did, despite all his or her

ebullience, provide a most concise version of the legend of
Ringing Rocks and the baseline for the beliefs of some latter-

*It is upon this rock that the ghostly legend of Ringing Rocks is
believed to have had its origins.*

73

day mystics that from those boulders whirls a vortex of supernatural forces.

The legend follows a familiar form. Its principals are Atchokatha and Namechi, a pair of star-crossed Lenni-Lenape lovers who were caught in a cultural cross-fire at Ringing Rocks so long ago.

The warrior Atchokatha had fallen in love with the maiden Namechi, but their tribes were feuding.

Still, the couple vowed to overcome their elders' differences and express their love to one another. That love was to be sealed forever at the rocks which, according to the legend, ring as an eternal echo of their doomed affair.

The field of rocks was the place the two would rendezvous regularly during times of tension between the tribes.

But one day, those tensions boiled over to war. On a day when Atchokatha was to meet Namechi at the rocks, the war councils of their respective tribes were to engage in battle.

Only the lovers knew of their appointment together. And, while Namechi went to the rocks in sweet innocence, her beloved Atchokatha was there with his fellow warriors to meet their enemy.

I quote from the anonymous chronicler's account:

Not heeding the warning of the tribesman, Atchokatha bounded over the huge rock masses until he reached the great boulder which sits in the center, on which in the past he had often waited many happy moments for the coming of the soft-eyed Namechi.

Would she come to him now? Suddenly, he caught the flutter of her garments as she climbed over the rocks to greet him where he stood with outstretched hands.

There was a harsh twang of a bow string, the flight of an arrow, and a messenger of Namechi's people proved fleeter than Namechi, and the breast of the young warrior was stained with blood.

He stood erect, though he had received a death wound, until the faithful Namechi had reached him and had been clasped to

MONTGOMERY COUNTY GHOST STORIES

his bleeding breast.

Just then another arrow winged its way from the bow of Atchokatha's brother who, having seen his kinsman bleed, smote the beautiful Namechi. With a sigh, her spirit fled.

For an instant Atchokatha stood there, proud and defiant, with his loved one in his arms, while below and around him continued the war-whoop and battle. Then, as his limbs grew weak, his fingers, which clasped the tomahawk, relaxed, and his weapon fell with a crash on the great surface of the rock.

There was a sound like a bell that startled the warriors and stayed every hand. The two forms swayed an instant, and Atchokatha, with the beautiful Namechi in his arms, plunged down to death, while clear and sweet above them echoed the strange, weird music from the rock.

From that day, when for the first time the rocks sang so sweetly, the Indians reverenced them.

But, there's more!

In the October 31, 1970 edition of *the Pottstown Mercury*, respected historian W. Edmunds Claussen presented to the newspaper readers a story headlined: "HOBGOBLINS ACTIVE AT RINGING ROCKS."

Claussen deferred to *a Pottstown Ledger* article which had been published almost a century before.

The story, by *Ledger* editor L.H. Davis, recounted that writer's account of a journey to the Ringing Hill Hotel and the famed Ringing Rocks.

Davis perpetuated the overblown melodic qualities of the rocks. "When struck by a hammer or stone, they gave forth a clear, metallic ring like that of a blacksmith's anvil, or as in some sort of the finest ringers, like a large bell."

He also further clouded the geological genesis of the boulder field. "The loose boulders scattered over the surface for a great distance," Davis wrote, "can only be accounted for on the theory that they have been hurled there from the crater of a volcano."

Davis also recorded a long-standing tale of the supposedly haunted limekilns which dotted the land around Ringing Hill.

75

"In those days," he said, "when superstition was more rife than in our enlightened day; when every old house or barn had its ghost story connected with it; when people saw men without heads; when lights were carried about without hands; and noises unearthly were heard without any human agency, these limekilns were frequently the scenes of hobgoblin apparitions."

He cited one in particular. "The story is told of the old kiln on the Bliem (sic) farm, on the Swamp Road near the Ringing Hill Hotel, that strange lights and queer noises were frequently heard emanating from the old kiln, and people had come to consider it haunted."

Still today, some people who live in the area surrounding Ringing Rocks believe that the spirits of fallen Indians may roam the rocks and beyond.

One property owner who asked to not be identified said she has seen eerie, glowing forms rising from the Ringing Rocks and has always felt that the place had a magical charm.

"I heard the stories about ghosts," she said. "I never put a lot of faith in them. But, I must admit that there is some kind of eeriness about the rocks, and this whole area. I could swear that, a few times when I was walking around the rocks, I saw misty-like figures in the distance. But, they could have been anything but ghosts.

"And, if they are, so be it. The place certainly must have been strange to the Indians, and probably was something they held in some kind of reverence.

"So, maybe it is their ghosts that really do remain here. Like I said, so be it. It's nice to live near a place with legends like that."

Gwynedd Tunnel, Gwynedd Valley, Pa.

The Gwynned Tunnel in the early 20th century.

The Fright at the End of the Tunnel

For this story, we consulted a series of newspaper articles and an account published in no less an impressive ledger as the Bulletin of the Historical Society of Montgomery County.

It is the story of a dish-smashing, mirror-shattering, pot-heaving poltergeist that pestered a Gwynned family for a week in September, 1886.

So incredible and unexplained was the experience that word of it spread across the country and folks from miles around gathered to hear what they could hear and see what they could see.

The setting was a house just west of DeKalb Street and quite near the Gwynned Tunnel which carried through it the lines of the Bethlehem Branch of the Reading Railroad.

Its occupants were identified as Mr. and Mrs. Frank D. Worley, their 12-year old daughter and sons Frank and Matthew. Mr. Worley was described as the former treasurer of the Commercial Exchange in Philadelphia.

It was Friday, September 24 when Mrs. Worley and the children were sitting in their living room. Without notice, their solitude was split apart by the sound of something crashing in the cellar.

As the 16-year old Frank scurried downstairs, Mrs. Worley already had her suspicions as to what might have been the matter.

She had some 250 jars of preserves stored on shelves in the cellar, and she feared that some of their contents had fermented and blown the tops off the jars.

In the cellar, they did find about 50 jars scattered and broken on the floor. As a precaution, mother had the children gather the remaining jars and take them to the kitchen where she would reheat the preserves and put the messy issue to rest.

But, doubt was cast into Mrs. Worley's theory as several jars which had been placed on the kitchen table simply moved and hurled themselves to the floor.

Standing back and watching in disbelief, Mrs. Worley, her daughter and young Frank were aghast. Matthew had heard his father coming home and went into the front yard to greet him and tell him of their experience.

As Matthew and his father stood in the yard, they watched incredulously as a jar of preserves...another....and then another....crashed through the cellar window!

There was no way to explain it. It was not fermentation.

Throughout the weekend more jars burst or bolted. In the summer kitchen a large soup tureen stood on end and burst. Mirrors broke from their centers. Glass in picture frames cracked and split apart. A window crumbled into shards of rubble.

Word of the Worleys' woes spread quickly around the neighborhood. Witness after witness corroborated and chronicled the events–a continuing parade of broken cups, glass chimneys rising and flying through windows to points 50 feet and farther in the yard, leaping teacups, and crashing crockery.

MONTGOMERY COUNTY GHOST STORIES

For several days, sporadic incidents took place as friends and neighbors struggled to explain and to help.

One neighbor, William Boyer, took a tough-guy stance. As he and the elder Frank Worley sat in the house, they both watched a teacup slide from a table to the floor. It did not break. Both times, Boyer put it back on the table. The second time, he commanded, "Now, stay there!"

The cup stayed. For a few seconds. Then, it slid, fell, and broke.

Even several pieces of a dish set given to Mr. Worley by the Commercial Exchange were broken in the poltergeists' free-for-all.

The Historical Society article noted that large crowds eventually gathered around the afflicted property. "Parties were made up throughout the surrounding country to drive to the Worley house in haywagons and watch for the ghosts. Visitors also came on railroad trains from Philadelphia and elsewhere."

While the astounding events continued through six full days, it was on the seventh and last day of the phenomenon when some of the wildest activity took place.

According to the Historical Society publication:

At noon that day Matthew Worley was holding a small china platter in his hand when it began to move on a circle. He let go of it and it flew through a window, falling thirty feet away.

A platter two feet long, one-quarter of an inch thick and weighing several pounds rose from a table and shot through a window being broken into eleven pieces as it fell.

Six oil lamps fell from a chandelier in two rooms, and that night the family had to burn candles for illumination.

And, that turned out to be the final incident of the near-week long spectacle.

A vigil was kept on Friday, but all the sinister activity ceased.

As the family counted its losses and prayed that nothing else would happen, a level of normalcy returned to the Worley household.

79

The flocks of the curious dwindled and departed. Mrs. Worley, who had been driven to despair by the astonishing and thoroughly unexplainable experience, was calmed.

Neighbors gathered to attempt to rationalize the ordeal and center on any possible culprits.

Some blamed it on a "magnetism" that spun from and around the couple's adopted daughter. Mrs. Worley profoundly rejected that idea.

Others said it was simply the repercussions of recent blasting in the nearby Gwynned Tunnel.

But, the nature of the events was not consistent with that possibility and no one could fix or match the times of the rampages with the times of the blasting.

In the end, the entire community scratched its collective head with confusion.

As recent as 1944, the matter was brought up once again in a Norristown newspaper.

The story recalled the 19th century appearances of "magnetizers" and "hypnotizers" who came to Norristown and dazzled a bewildered public with their "talents."

Those gentlemen, including "Jackson, the Celebrated Magnetizer" who appeared in town in 1841 and "Herr Dreisbach" who dropped by three years later, were medicine show performers who "mesmerized" and "hypnotized" entire crowds of people. The latter set up shop on grounds now occupied by the old county prison.

The writer admitted that the "magnetizers" were probably effecting a kind of "mass hysteria," but was cautious in regards to the Worley incident.

"Scarcely any other similar experience was better vouched for than this series of amazing occurrences," the writer noted.

"By trying to explain the case as being due to mass hysteria, it was necessary to assume that all the people who saw the flying objects and the breakage did not really see such things but merely imagined they did because everybody was talking about the case.

"Another attempt at explanation was to hold a

MONTGOMERY COUNTY GHOST STORIES

mischievous son of the Worleys responsible. If one small boy could keep up such a demonstration for two weeks that would have been even more marvelous than if the cause had been mass hysteria."

Was it the act of poltergeists or some other heinous supernatural beings? Was it the act of a young boy? Was it mass hysteria?

Who will ever know for certain? The Gwynned Ghost remains one of Montgomery County's most enduring mysteries.

81

Is Hope Lodge Haunted?

There is no easy answer to the above question.

What is known is that Hope Lodge is a survivor–the survivor of its own planned demolition and its all-encompassing suburban sprawl.

Saved from the wrecker's ball by William and Alice Degn in the early 1900s, Hope Lodge has been hailed as a prime example of Georgian architecture. Its interior has been "adjusted" over its many transitions before the property was taken over by the state in 1957.

Built by Quaker merchant Samuel Morris between 1743 and 1748, Hope Lodge has a rich history as well as a few mysteries–including, they say, some ghosts.

The "they" in this case are past and present staff and board members and a visitor or two who has been caught off-guard by ghostly goings-on there.

During the Revolution, the William West family resided there, and while Colonial troops camped just over the hill at Whitemarsh after the Battle of Germantown and before their deployment to Valley Forge, the mansion was "borrowed" to serve as the headquarters of Surgeon Gen. John Cochran.

The property was purchased later by Henry Hope, a European banker and financier who became owner-in-absentia. Hope then gave it to his nephew, Horatio Watmough, as a wedding present. Watmough gave the place its present name in honor of his uncle.

Incidentally, another notable item is named after that same Hope family–the Hope Diamond!

For a period of about 90 years, the property was farmed and the handsome mansion was relegated to being a farmhouse. Little was done to improve and modernize the building in that time, and in the 1920s, the home was scheduled to be demolished to make room for the expansion of an adjacent limestone quarry. It was saved from the wrecker's ball by the Degns, who revitalized the aging home within its traditional architectural bounds.

And, within those walls now dwell many legends and, as the author of the Lodge World Wide Web pages calls them, "myths."

The site attempts to debunk several anecdotal tales by stating, "While the stories...as told by long-time local residents of the area...are continually interesting, there is absolutely no evidence to substantiate any of them."

Still, the author concedes their importance. "They are reported," the site continued, "because to fully appreciate any historic site, you should know its myths."

One of those myths mentioned was: There are reports of ghosts of soldiers who died in this house when it "was a hospital" during the Whitemarsh encampment of 1777.

Myth? Perhaps. Still, the stories persist that at least one Colonial soldier did perish during surgery in the cellar of the Lodge, and his moaning, anguished spirit continues to trod the lowest level of the building.

What's more, there was a story a while back that for decades–perhaps as long a century after his death there–a stain from his blood remained on the basement floor. Any and all attempts to wash it, scrape it, or remove it in any way were for naught.

That blood stain, and for the most part that story, have since faded into the haze of history.

But, Patty Mousley, who shares responsibilities as museum educator at Graeme Park and Hope Lodge, did remember at least one person who commented on seeing a phantom figure there. "I do recall," she said, "that a visitor told me they were in the parlor closing up and they thought they saw the form by the desk."

So, any spirit activity there seems weak, and its authenticity in question.

But, with its interesting and enticing history, Hope Lodge seems to beg for more intense psychic investigation which may indeed turn up more substantial paranormal phenomena.

Evidence of a spirit at the F.O.E. Post 626, Pottstown?

An Apparition at the Eagles

What was the old Grant School building in Pottstown has, since the 1970s, been Post 626 of the Fraternal Order of Elks.

A walk beyond the comfortable clubhouse barroom will reveal an aging structure with many architectural foibles and challenges.

84

Upstairs and downstairs, the building shows its age and seems to hold within its walls many secrets of its many years and many transitions.

And, several F.O.E. members believe, the old school harbors a ghost or two.

Eric Witte, a former officer, said he once heard the mysterious sound of footsteps running across the floor, trailing off from the middle of the bar area toward a door to the outside. As that sound perked his ears, he distinctly heard a door open and close, as if whoever–or whatever– was running across the room made its escape.

What baffled him, however, was that he knew he was absolutely alone in the club at the time, and all outer doors were locked. No door could have opened, and no door could have closed.

Witte's experience was the tip of the ethereal iceberg at the Eagles' club.

Several members we spoke two in a "reading" of the building said they truly believed one or more entities inhabited the four floors of the old school building.

Richard "Doc" Soos has felt otherworldly presences in the bar area, and linked the aroma of fresh-brewed coffee with the coming of the spirits he feels he has sensed.

From bartenders to barstool warmers, folks at the Eagles are not frightened of the ghosts there, but they are somewhat confused.

Dot Clifford, whose late husband tended bar there, told of the time her husband was counting money after the club had closed for the night. His eyes were distracted by the sight of a mysterious man sitting in a chair near the pool table.

"My husband said the man was dressed all in gray, like an old-fashioned military uniform," Dot said.

Puzzled as to how the man might have gotten there and knowing he shouldn't have been there, Mr. Clifford started around the bar to tell the chap he'd have to leave.

As he did so, the man in gray silently vanished before the bartender's astonished eyes.

MONTGOMERY COUNTY GHOST STORIES

An apparition matching the description given by Clifford has been spotted by at least one other bartender.

An investigation of the building did reveal several "hot spots" of possible paranormal activity. One particular chamber, deep in the corner of the basement, seemed to be the center of much of that activity–as if it was inhabited by an invisible, benign, but powerful force.

And, several photographs taken by the investigators revealed some interesting anomalies.

Debbi Kerr, who accompanied the author on several cases, caught several abnormalities on film, the most amazing being several white shafts of light which seemed to have a spiraling pattern. The pictures were taken in areas thought by F.O.E. members to be "hot spots" of paranormal activity.

Another photograph of the exterior front of the building revealed a slash of light which streamed across the exposure–in only one frame of several which were taken at the same time.

Do these pictures serve as photographic evidence that the Eagles' home is haunted? Are these pictures of ghosts?

Several professional photographers and processors examined the pictures and could come up with no logical explanation.

Maybe, just maybe, there is none.

Maybe, just maybe, they indeed are pictures...of ghosts.

📖

The supernatural is as instant to those of us who live in back country places as it was in medieval times to our ancestors in Germany–Cornelius Weygandt, English Literature Professor, University of Pennsylvania. From his book, *The Red Hills: A Record of Good Days Outdoor and In, With Things Pennsylvania Dutch* (University of Pennsylvania Press, 1929)

*Does a woman in colonial dress haunt this room
at Pottsgrove Manor?*

Manifestation at the Manor

John Potts wouldn't recognize the old place.

All right, the ironmaster and patriarch of the patriotic Potts clan might find his old Georgian mansion somewhat familiar, but if he made a 360-degree scan of his old homestead he'd be confused, at the very least.

In his time, Potts could stand on his back porch and look over broad meadows toward northern hills. From the front entranceway he could survey his holdings clear to the Schuylkill River.

Today, the Pottsgrove Manor house is almost smothered by streets, highways, and rail yards. It has been pushed by Pottstown and shoved by Stowe.

The views John Potts would have today are a bit gritty. If he would try to find his barn today, he would have to look under the asphalt of a parking lot.

What was a true manor of more than a thousand acres has been whittled down to a little more than four.

A wide lawn rises rapidly from High Street, and the sandstone mansion stands proudly at its summit as it has since 1752.

So magnificent was John Potts' place when it was constructed that folks ambled all the way from Philadelphia and other towns just to gaze at the elegant residence.

Upon John's death in 1768, son Thomas Potts–one of John and Ruth Potts' 13 children–inherited the homestead. Thomas brought even more prestige to the family name.

He served at the 1776 Pennsylvania Constitutional Convention and as a colonel in the Revolutionary War. He was among the first to join Benjamin Franklin in his American Philosophical Society.

Thomas sold the property in 1783, and for more than 150 years it remained outside of Potts family ownership.

Just after the Civil War, the plantation had been pared to 275 acres, and the old home which had once been favorably compared with the mansions of Germantown, was in decline.

After a spell as the Mill Park Hotel, Pottsgrove Manor faced even more shame. Eventually, it became a ramshackled haven for rail-ridin' hobos.

In 1941, descendants of the original owner purchased what was left of the estate and immediately turned it over to the Pennsylvania Historic and Museum Commission.

The transition from tenement to tourist attraction was a juxtaposition of hard work and good fortune. Somehow, most of the splendid interior woodwork survived and the building was structurally sound.

In 1952, its bicentennial year, a restored Pottsgrove Manor opened for tours.

Now maintained by the county's superb Department of History and Cultural Arts, Pottsgrove Manor plays host to school groups, historical students, tourists....and a ghost or two.

And, for the stories of the manifestations in the manor, we spoke with William Brobst, the assistant administrator.

MONTGOMERY COUNTY GHOST STORIES

A native of Nazareth, Northampton County, Brobst had worked in historic sites for more than a dozen years. Prior to taking the post at Pottsgrove, he was employed at Hope Lodge and Pennypacker Mills–two other historic (and, some say, *haunted*) sites in Montgomery County.

When he first came to Pottsgrove Manor, he seemed to feel something a bit unusual on the staircase that leads from the second to the third floors.

"It was a presence," he said, "as if someone was looking over my shoulder. I never saw anything, but it felt as if something was there, really close behind me."

Bill Brobst was not alone. Others, including volunteers and staff, had also expressed their uneasiness as they walked that staircase to the third floor, which was once the slave quarters of the manor.

But, something else was to happen to Bill Brobst– something that would forever alter his attitudes about the supernatural, and his appreciation of Pottsgrove Manor.

"I'm almost embarrassed to talk about it," he continued, "because my senses say 'this is what I saw' but the human part of me says no, that's strange, people will think you're odd."

As he juggled his sensibilities and sensitivities, the articulate Mr. Brobst discussed his sighting with others, including site administrator Robert Study. As he did so, and they listened with empathy, his confidence grew and he agreed to share his story with the readers of this book.

The time of his experience was early in the morning around the 1999 Christmas holiday season. He had opened up the manor house with one other staff member. They were the only ones in the building, and they were literally locked inside. The manor was not opened to the public that day.

"I happened to be opening up the house," Brobst said. "The last room I usually get to is the children's bed chamber.

"All of a sudden I heard what sounded to be furniture being moved. It was a rustling sound, I thought it was the

89

other person here."

What was very strange about that sound was that it would likely never be heard there. It was the wood-on-wood sound of furniture being dragged across a bare floor. And that, Brobst knew, was a no-no with tenders of historic properties.

"As it turned out," Brobst continued, "I checked and that other person here was in her office. She had heard the sound too–and she thought it was *me*!

"So, I was at the children's bed chamber when I heard this.

"Then, I came out of the children's chamber. And as I did so, this image moved from the hallway into the master bed chamber.

"It was very close to the door, so I didn't get to see much. But, it was like you and I would have been standing there. It wasn't some smoky, shadowy form, anything like that. It was quite real.

"At first I thought it might have been one of our living historians, but no, I'd never seen that outfit before."

And besides, he noted, he was absolutely certain that he and his co-worker were the only living beings in that house, and every exterior door was locked.

Brobst provided a remarkably vivid description of the vision.

"It was definitely a female–a female of the upper class, of somebody who had money. I saw the back of her. She had light, brown, hair–almost to her shoulders. It was in tight curls, and she wore no cap.

"Her hair was very well coifed. I'd say she was about five foot-seven. The garment she was wearing was definitely early to mid-18th century. I didn't see her face, didn't see her skin, but I could tell from the cuffs and the pattern that her dress was of that period.

"It was a dark green gown, but it had flowers on it. I could tell that it was multi-colored damask fabric, or it was embroidered. And, she was definitely wearing a bustle that made her back end stick out.

"I was so dumbfounded that I had to catch my breath.

"Rather than calling out or saying anything I just walked across the second floor hall to that room.

"There was nothing. And at that point, I was very...."

Well, at *that* point in the interview, Bill Brobst drew a deep breath and gathered his thoughts. The experience of that December morning was obviously so powerful that to this day he is uncomfortable relating to it and attempting to rationalize it.

"Sometimes," he continued, with words broken by emotion, "I don't believe it myself!"

Returning to that day, that room, and that encounter, Bill continued.

"I just looked around the bed chamber to make sure that everything was where it was. Now, I'm pretty good at that because when I place something and anybody moves it, I know! And, nobody moved anything there.

"I tried to brush it all off. You know, like, *this is crazy*. I wasn't going to say anything to anybody. But, I came into the office and I was beside myself.

"I kept it to myself, but my co-worker detected something. She asked me what was wrong.

"I said, 'promise you don't say anything, but...'"

With that, he disclosed the details of the incident. And with that, he began to deal with what had happened.

"From past experiences," he said, "and from what other volunteers had said, I felt like I was in good company. But at that point, I wasn't really ready to talk about it."

But, as he sorted out his thoughts and his words during our interview, one declaration was strong and conclusive.

"I guess what I'm saying," he said–his eyes now resolute and his face affixed, "is that I am a believer. There is something here."

As Bill Brobst is not alone in that belief, the colonial woman whose spirit shuffled silently into the second floor bed chamber may not be alone as a haunter of the manor house.

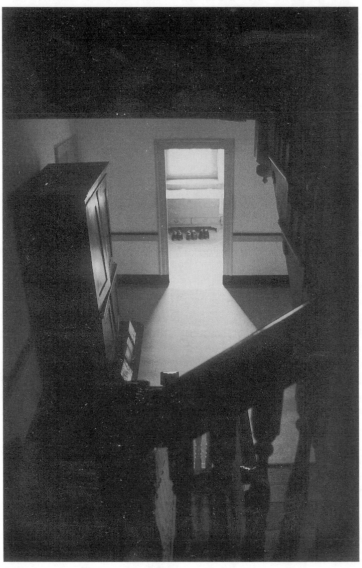

Some people have experienced unsettling sensations on this staircase at Pottsgrove Manor.

MONTGOMERY COUNTY GHOST STORIES

One volunteer has spotted the ghost of a man who sits at a desk by a window in the building's work room. Another individual has shared Bill's feelings on the staircase between the second and third floors.

But, ever since his experience, Bill is cautious and on guard.

"I'll tell you," he told us, "before I walk into that room now, I kind of prepare myself."

His range of emotions had now run to nervous chuckles as he recalled that fateful day.

"Now, it's always like I kind of don't want to believe. It's stupid. Shut up. People will think I'm crazy.

"But, I will never doubt my senses on that one–what I saw that morning."

Pottsgrove Manor.

93

The original farmhouse at the Joseph Ambler Inn.

Jonathan

It is a pleasant, almost unexpected grove of trees wedged between suburban commercial sprawl and clusters of condos and townhouses.

And, despite the bucolic trappings and the sylvan insulation provided by what's left of the Little Neshaminy Creek watershed on that edge of Montgomery County, the muffled roar of nearby traffic and a marbled sky streaked by lineal layers of jet contrails reminded us of where we were.

Once inside the quiet enclave, however, more noticeable were the flocks of crows that fluttered by—and one ominous blackbird that perched itself at the very top of the tallest tree.

Beneath it, rustling in a bed of fallen autumn leaves, a squirrel went about its business. The November sun cast

94

crisp shadows on the fieldstone house and barn.

There were certainly stories to be told here at the Joseph Ambler Inn. But, were there *ghost* stories?

It was what research partner Dave Seibold and I refer to as a "cold call." We would present ourselves and inquire as to the presence of any presences. It's a craps shoot–more often than we land a good ghost story we find nothing, or are sent packing as those we have called upon chortle or chastise us for even inferring that their inn, their restaurant, their historic site, or their B&B could harbor ghosts.

At that place, that Joseph Ambler Inn, there would be no chortling, no chastising. There would be a ghost story, and a good one.

The Joseph Ambler Inn is all of the above–an inn, a restaurant, historical site, and a bed and breakfast.

The inn's namesake was a weelwright on the William Morgan estate in the early 18th century. In 1741, Morgan's family deeded 160 acres of that estate to Ambler and his wife, Ann.

The farmhouse which now stands as the centerpiece of the inn was built in 1734 and is the oldest building on the grounds.

After generations of ownership within the Ambler family (including a brief period during which Mary Ambler, the legendary namesake of the nearby borough, owned it), the farm went into the hands of a succession of owners.

In 1982, the transition from farm to inn was made, and since then many improvements and expansions have taken place.

The most remarkable and unusual expansion took place in the summer of 1997 when a 225-ton newcomer arrived.

It is the Thomas Wilson House, which was moved three miles down Horsham Road and put in place in a corner of the Joseph Ambler Inn's 12 acres. Built in the mid-1800s, the two-story stone home was saved from demolition and laboriously relocated with much fanfare (and many dollars). It now houses ten of the inn's more than three dozen guest rooms and suites.

So again, there must be many stories here. But what about those *ghost* stories?

For them, we turned to innkeeper Terry Kratz.

She walked us through the charming inn and into the nooks and crannies where many who work, stay, or dine there say that spirits roam.

We settled into the "School Room," a comfortable common room in which Terry schooled us as to the otherworldly occurrences that unfold from time to time all around us–and, from our vantage point–literally right over our heads.

"I know that people talk about seeing someone in the Wolf Room," Terry said, referring to one of two small rooms in the uppermost floor of an addition to the farmhouse.

"That would have, at some time, been an attic," she continued. "Sometime in the 1920s, it was a girls' dormitory. It was then one open space. When we came, we divided it into two separate rooms."

It should be noted that the Wolf Room is probably no more, since as this book was being written, a wall between the Wolf and Wright rooms was being removed to create one, larger room on that third-floor once again.

And, in what was the Wolf Room there was a chair–a chair they came to call the "Thinker's Chair."

It earned that moniker because of wooden ringlets which are positioned at the end of each arm of the chair. It's assumed the ringlets were placed their for fidgeting, or *thinking*. Well, that's the assumption.

"It's like a folding, wooden camp chair," Terry said. "And people have said that they have awakened in the morning or the night and have seen someone sitting in that chair."

That third-floor room has been the setting for several sightings over the years. "I've never heard of anyone coming screaming away from the room," Terry added, "but sure,

The "Thinker's Chair" at the Joseph Ambler Inn.
97

some people might be creeped out by the idea of a 'haunted room.'"

But, as we have found in our other books set in such B&B-rich areas as Bucks County and Cape May, many people actually seek out these places and those rooms.

The fact that the walls have come down on the third floor and the two small rooms have once again been opened up to form one larger chamber may well suit one spirit who has not only been seen at the Joseph Ambler Inn, but who has also been given a name.

He is "Jonathan," and he was first identified by a pair of self-proclaimed "sensitives" who dropped by one day in 1994 and forever changed everyday life at the inn.

Wanda Dezzi, meeting coordinator at the Joseph Ambler, explained.

"Two ladies came by the front desk when it was in the barn," she said. "They asked if we minded if they walked around the property. We said it was all right.

"They came back to the front desk and they said that in the house, on the third floor, there was a presence that was very unhappy because the room had been divided and that parties were held here."

That presence could be seen sitting in the "Thinker's Chair."

The "sensitives," or mediums, had no prior knowledge of any previous supernatural activity at the inn. They knew nothing of any prior sightings of mysterious forms in *the chair*.

They told Wanda and others that the spirit on the third floor was discontent, but not threatening in any way. And, he was not alone in the psychic plane of the inn.

"One of the women," Wanda continued, "said there was a presence at the entrance to the barn. And, it started to get a little weird. Her body language changed, she started to talk like a man, and it was then that she said the presence's name there was Jonathan."

Wanda said the medium described Jonathan as an "earthy" type, probably a farmer.

98

"She said he also was not threatening, or anything like that, but he really didn't like it when people at the front desk weren't working diligently. He wanted to see people working!"

And while to this day, Jonathan's work ethic might help spur employees to high levels of proficiency and efficiency, his ghostly presence more often gets the blame for anything untoward or unexplained that might happen around the property.

Another haunted place on the grounds is the Corybeck, a detached, ca. 1929 cottage with four rooms and a suite.

In the late 1990s, a couple was occupying one of those rooms. In the wee hours of the morning, the woman awakened to witness the ghostly image of another woman, clad in Colonial-style dress and bonnet, calmly pouring water from a pitcher into a bowl.

As mysteriously as she had appeared, she disappeared. The befuddled guest drew a few deep breaths, tried her best to reason with what she had seen, managed to get back to sleep, and rose the next morning with an experience she will never forget and never be able to explain.

Another inn employee is keenly aware of the eternal guests who ramble the Ambler. But, Terry Peck, the night manager, concurs that they are universally friendly.

And, the tender of the graveyard shift at the inn corroborates her co-workers' stories. Throughout her overnight hours she has heard numerous reports of odd activities in all four buildings.

"I've had guests come down at three in the morning in their bathrobes and slippers, telling me they have had experiences."

An amiable and gracious hostess, Terry cleverly assuages the guests' anxieties, especially when they ask her, point-blank, if there are ghosts in the inn.

With that, she sets up a sort of a Russian Roulette response.

"I tell them there are reports of ghosts here, but not in

their room."

Terry Peck recalled several incidents. "It's just that all of a sudden there's a feeling, or a face," she noted. "Then, it's over."

She said one particular story she recalls came from a guest who told her that while he was shaving, he glanced in the mirror and saw, standing behind him, another person in the room. But, when he wheeled around to see who was there, no one was!

Terry admits she has never had any encounters with the spirits of the inn. But, she does not reject the notion.

"I would love to meet the ghosts," she mused as we spoke at about 4:30 a.m., "I could use the company!"

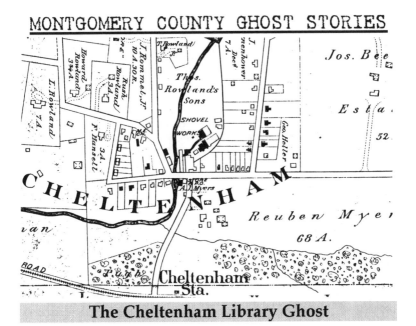

The Cheltenham Library Ghost

Anyone with more than a little gray around their temples who grew up in the Cheltenham area will recall the stories of what was that area's most famous ghost story– the ghost of the old East Cheltenham Free Library.

The building is long gone, replaced by a three-sided gravel parking lot owned by the township and occupied by customers for neighboring businesses.

The library was replaced by its current facility at Myrtle and Elm Avenues.

But, it was on that vacant lot at Central Avenue and Old Soldiers Road, at the foot of Tookany Creek Parkway where the stories were told, the seances were held, and the ghosts walked.

There, in Cheltenham Village, on the very edge of the county, is where the more seasoned of local citizens will remember not only their pleasant trips to the library, but the stories of its haunting.

"I used to take my children there," said Anita Griffiths.

101

"It was a wonderful place for kids. It was like going into a real house."

Anita, once a patron of the old library and more recently an assistant at the "new" one, admitted that she never had any personal encounter with the ghosts. "But," she continued, "I had once said to one of the ladies there, once I got to know them, that there was something strange about the bottom of the stairs. I would get a feeling, that's all. There was always something there.

"They asked me if I knew about the ghost. I said no, I hadn't read or heard anything about the story.

"That's when they told me about the coffee and all that."

Betty Adams also heard the stories. She spoke of a hanging that took place in a garage to the rear of the old library and other unusual deaths that occurred in or around the building.

As for the ghost, Betty said, "We always figured the ghost story was probably from the time when it was a store, or when it was a chocolate factory and a lady fell through the floor there."

Indeed, the old library building, a simple but handsome structure, was built in the early 1800s. In 1866, it became a general store and its proprietor, Albert J. Myers, became postmaster and established the post office there.

John and James Houldin operated a general store there in 1906, and throughout the first half of the 20th century it served as a store and in other capacities.

In 1959, the township bought the building and leased it to the library.

As one of the oldest buildings in Cheltenham Township at that time, the building was held in a certain reverence by local historians.

It was in the 1940s when the ghostly activity started to surface. But, it would remain only as a quiet local legend until the late 1960s when the story was discussed more openly.

The Evening Bulletin, a Philadelphia daily newspaper,

MONTGOMERY COUNTY GHOST STORIES

was among the first publications to bring the story to public light.

An article in January, 1970 quoted the head librarian, who confessed that she had no interest nor belief in the supernatural, but had heard the stories. "Our ghost isn't the malevolent sort," Mrs. John Bockman said, "It's simply a quiet, coffee-brewing, dinner-cooking spook."

And, that seems to have been the prevailing popular account of the ghost of the old library. But, there would eventually be many more details–and ghosts–revealed.

In the 1970 article, Mrs. Bockman said it was about 4:30 in the afternoon when, on occasion, the distinct aroma of freshly-brewed coffee and/or the smell of cooking was detected, "...like the smell of cooking in anyone's kitchen at meal time," according to Mrs. Bockman.

"We became so used to it that we simply commented to each other, 'Mrs. Houldin is cooking her dinner!'"

It should be noted, and indeed *was* noted by the staunchly skeptical Mrs. Bockman, that the library windows were hermetically sealed and there was no other building–or kitchen–anywhere on the block.

What's more, there was no kitchen, and no coffee pot, in the library.

At that time, 17-year old library aide Betsy Stratton told the *Bulletin* reporter that she was once on the second floor of the oldest section of the building when she heard a very clear snorting sound.

She paused and listened. The snort came again, and again. "So," she said, "I snorted right back! It answered, and so did I. We kept that up, over and over again, until I got tired and walked away."

The *Bulletin* was back in June, 1971, this time to cover a walk-through by several psychics and mediums from regional paranormal investigation groups.

Mrs. Bockman, still rejecting the notion of ghosts, was nonetheless a gracious hostess.

One of the investigators took very few steps inside the front door before he proclaimed the building "haunted."

103

He almost immediately identified a female spirit in a polka-dot dress and a tall, 30-ish male in the second floor periodical room.

Most ominous was another unfortunate ghost on the second floor. "I get the vision of a body burned to a crisp in the library," the anonymous investigator was quoted as saying.

And so, the ghost stories about the old library reached a fever's pitch around Cheltenham–and far, far beyond. The Philadelphia Parks and Recreation Department went as far as including the "haunted library" on some tour itineraries.

In December, 1976, the story was presented to the world in a rather fatuous feature in the *National Enquirer*.

That ignominious article was to be one of the last hurrahs for the old ghost of the old library. The library moved to its present location fewer than three blocks away and the old store/butcher shop/chocolate factory/post office/etc./etc. was abandoned and demolished.

But before the historic building went down (at the behest of the state department of transportation to create a safer traffic pattern–something that never really happened), everybody and anybody who had heard the stories or smelled the coffee or stew or pot roast or whatever tried one last time to rationalize and explain those stories and experiences.

Nobody really could.

And to this day, if one were to stand on that triangular lot where the library once stood, would one get a whiff of coffee? See the ghostly form of a woman in a polka-dot dress? Exchange snorts with an unseen snorter?

Who knows?

What is known is that although the library and the building are no more, the story of the ghosts of the old East Cheltenham Library is truly one for the books.

MONTGOMERY COUNTY GHOST STORIES

The Reaper Ghost Along the Schuylkill

Well before the first European settlers came to Montgomery County, the Schuylkill River was already established as a vital lifeline for trade and travel.

Now, Pennsylvania's first official "Scenic River" is a recreational delight. It at once forms Montgomery County's southern boundary and divides the county.

And, its banks, islands and waters are not without their bizarre and unexplainable events.

Take, for example, the documented June, 1878 case of "Sinky" Bechtel and Billy Reinard, who had some most unsettling nights on the shore of the river near Savage Rock, described then as "a few miles below Pottstown."

The men were harvesting sandy soil from the river bank and loading it into their wagons. They, and their dog, camped in a covered wagon overnight during their job assignment.

A story in the *Daily Ledger* provided its readers with details divulged by Reinard.

"At about the same hour each night," the newspaper writer said, "he heard supernatural voices, and these were succeeded by a vision of spectral horses, four in number, drawing a spectral mowing or reaping machine accompanied by three or four short, square-built men, all passing down the river just above the water. But though the machine appeared to be in motion, no sound of its clattering wheels, levers, or cutting bar could be heard as it glided along and disappeared in the distance."

"Mr. Reinard does not pretend to account for this four-horse mower and reaper ghost. He says that he 'hadn't been taking anything' and that the vision appeared to him when he was wide awake and not in dreams."

The writer assured the readers that the story was written almost verbatim from Reinard's interview.

"One of the astonishing portions of the story," the

article continued, "is that the dog belonging to the party was thrown into such spasms of terror, according to Mr. Reinard's statement, that the hair on his back not only stood straight up, but turned the other way, and has remained so ever since!"

In addition to this rather odd and, some might say, delusory story, the article mentioned another interesting tale.

"The scene of the [Reinard] story is located not far away from where another supernatural occurrence took place several years ago.

"An aged farmer lost several horses by a disease that seemed to puzzle the veterinary surgeons, and everybody else, and only the theory that the animals were bewitched seemed to be a tenable one to account for their deaths.

"The farmer consulted a witch doctor, the Reading medicine man, no doubt, who told him to bore a hole in some part of the woodwork of his barn, drive a spike into the hole, and that would disenchant his horses and drive away the witches.

"He was enjoined to drive the spike gently. However, for fear if he hammered it in suddenly the witch would be killed. When the old man had bored the hole and started the spike, however, he gave it a tremendous whack that at once sent it home, thus disobeying his instructions.

"To complete the tale, it is said that an aged female, supposed to be that veritable witch, died in that vicinity the next day. After that the farmer's horses got well and were no longer bewitched."

📖

Ghosts of the Saylor Homestead

Any member of the Saylor family and most folks who live around the old Saylor homestead on the Linfield-Trappe Road know the story of the day George Washington came to call.

They say it was in September, 1777, when the general paused under a giant oak tree on at Henry Saylor's place.

And, when the genial Mr. Saylor ambled from his house to chat with the future president, a local legend was born.

But, there are more stories to be told about the old Saylor homestead. Ghost stories, that is.

The Saylor clan is one of the proud plankowners of Limerick Township. Henry Sr., who tarried with the good general in 1777 turned the property over to his son, Henry Jr., who added the post of Limerick Township assessor to his resume of "farmer." It was he who built the present farmhouse.

One of his sons, Albert, moved into Pottstown and opened a dry goods store in the mid-19th century.

Albert and Mary Ann Saylor had two children, including Henry Durston Saylor, who became a lawyer. In 1900, he was elected to represent his district in the Pennsylvania Senate. He also served in United States Consulates in Germany, Cuba, and the Yukon Territory.

Upon the death of Henry Saylor Jr. In 1877, the property was willed to another son, Azariah. He, in turn, deeded the farm to a nephew, Albert Reese Saylor, who lived there while forging a successful career as a pharmacist and manufacturer of remedies and patent medicines.

Through the first half of the 20th century, the old farmhouse fell into gradual disrepair. A fire in 1946 nearly destroyed it.

Twelve years later, with the building in dire straits,

Hon. Harold Durston Saylor, an attorney and Philadelphia Orphans Court judge, took charge and, with the help of a very handy tenant, rebuilt his family's homestead.

Through the next three decades, a succession of family members resided in and owned the property.

Enter Harold Durston Saylor II, son of the judge and himself a lawyer.

A ninth-generation Saylor, Harold told most of the tales of the unexplained and unexplainable in the house.

As a college student in the late 1970s, Harold spent some nights there on occasion. One particular night, about 11 o'clock, as he lay waiting to fall asleep, he heard footsteps coming up the staircase. He cautiously slipped out of bed, ventured to the top of the stairs, and saw nothing, no one.

He shook his head, went back to bed, settled in...and heard the footsteps once again.

He was confused, but not frightened. "It's only my family," he was quoted as saying. "They're the only ones who have ever owned the place. They're not going to bother me."

Following his graduation from college, Harold moved into the house in 1981. He would live there until the spring of 1984, and in those three years, several incidents left him shaking his head many more times.

Items would move. They'd disappear and reappear in unexpected places.

"The spirits were orderly and tidy," he said then. "They wanted everything right. It happened many times."

And then, there was more, much more.

There would be sounds, strange sounds. There would be such unnerving experiences as shelves of books literally flying from bookcases. There would be a bed, shaking, as if unseen hands were alerting Harold and his wife that their baby was crying–*which it was*–and they weren't hearing it–*which they weren't*–until the shaking bed awakened them.

Harold Saylor went on to buy the property from his

father's estate. He and his family moved there in April, 1988.

They are quite comfortable there. Never, even during the phantom footsteps/flying books/shaking bed episodes, were any of the encounters threatening.

And, Harold Saylor remains intrigued with the many mysteries of the property. He said that nobody is really sure, for example, where the patriarch of the Saylor family, Henry Sr., was buried. "It's somewhere on the property," he is fairly certain, "but the exact spot is anybody's guess."

And, as for the ghosts?

"Well," he conceded, "in the past ten years or so, there's been very little activity."

"Then again, maybe I'm just used to it!"

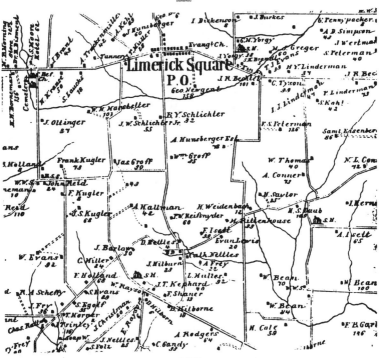

Sunrise Mill
The Whistling Indian of Sunrise Mill

When the waves of European settlers spread out across Montgomery County in the 18th century, among the first things they learned from the aboriginals of the land were their ancient legends and lore.

Along the old pathways and trails, rivers and streams, these stories were handed down to the newcomers by the natives.

Some of those tales have faded completely from history while others linger in dusty volumes deep in the files of libraries and historical societies.

Among them is the story of the ghost of Mill Hill–an Indian chief whose spirit is said to roam along Swamp Creek opposite Sunrise Mill.

The natives said that this ghost was the harbinger of ill fortune.

Most of the time, they said, the old chief rested quietly peacefully in his grave on the wooded, rocky ridge that rises high over creek and mill.

Most of the time, he was quiet.

But on occasion, late at night, a muffled, rustling sound would reverberate through the forest, followed by a clear whistling sound–the whistling of the old chief.

In his essay, "Indians of the Perkiomen Valley," Samuel Faust Jr. said, "All the surrounding settlers began more or less to believe in these forewarnings and quite often they heard him whistle in the middle of the night.

"Some claimed to have heard him before all the wars; the great Indian wars, the Revolution, War of 1812, the Mexican, and Civil wars."

Does the whistling Indian ghost of Mill Hill still roam that ridge?

Nowadays, the domain of his spirit is within the 200-acre Sunrise Mill property owned by the county.

Destined to be developed into a county park, the land which straddles Limerick and Upper and Lower Frederick townships includes a rebuilt circa-1845 stone bridge over Swamp Creek, Michael Krause's 1767 grist and sawmill that provided supplies for local farmers and for the Colonial troops who camped nearby during the Revolution, the former home of noted bronchoscopic pioneer Dr. Chevalier Jackson, and that ridge.

When interviewed for this book a tenant in the county-owned Jackson house reported minor mysteries there, but knew nothing of the legend of the whistling Indian.

Perhaps as that land, the placid mill pond, and a restored Sunrise Mill take their place among the county's premiere areas for recreation and relaxation, the trees on that ridge may someday rustle once more. A whistling sound may filter through the leaves, and the old chief will sound another warning!

The Snow Ghost of Willow Grove

It is sometimes inconceivable to imagine anything but the sprawling development of *now* when trying to conjure up the Montgomery County of *then*.

Certain parts of the county have been so built up for so long that all but certain natural geological formations that escaped the bulldozer and backhoes remain as reminders of the time when all the land was wild.

Likewise, the modern media has tainted and twisted our imaginations so that only those of us who can reject that *now* and transport ourselves to the *then* can any longer appreciate the time-honored stories that once circulated in these areas and titillated the folks who lived there.

One of those areas is Samson's Hill, near Willow Grove, and one of those stories is about a ghost who appeared as the snows appeared in the dead of winter.

The hill was a lonely place back in 1730. Only Samson Davis, for whom it was named, and one other settler had cabins on its summit.

One night, as daylight drained from a winter sky painted purple by the setting sun, the snows came.

Samson Davis and his neighbor braced themselves for the storm.

And, as the winds howled and the violet sky was rubbed gray by the gathering gloom, an old Indian made his way toward Samson's cabin seeking shelter.

Sampson Davis brusquely turned him away.

So, among the eerie outlines of twisted trees silhouetted crisply against the waning winter sunset, the Indian continued on to the other man's humble home.

He, too, gave no refuge.

As the disconsolate native frantically sought any kind of asylum from the fury which was imminent, the storm swept over the hill with a vengeance.

Having had no time to prepare and no adequate

cover, the man cowered in frigid fear.

For days, the blizzard bombarded Sampson's Hill. Not until after a full week did Sampson and his neighbor manage to burrow out of the piles of drifted snow. And not for several more weeks did the snow finally melt to reveal a grisly sight.

There, in a ravine just beyond the cabins, the frozen, contorted corpse of the old Indian was discovered. His flesh turned a blue-black by the ice and snow, the poor soul's eyes were open and affixed in a ghastly gaze.

In his book, *Local Sketches and Legends*, published in 1887, historian William J. Buck wrote of the legend that spun from the unfortunate incident.

"It shortly afterwards became rumored and was believed for a long time by several in the vicinity that on stormy, snowy nights of winter the Indian's spirit would make its appearance and keep vigils in and around the place of his death.

"Some, when the storm was most violent, said they had distinctly heard his wailings and upbraidings. Others related how they encountered a white-sheeted specter here at different times."

Buck noted that it had been handed down through the storytellers of the generations that the Indian had placed curses on the properties at which he was spurned, "...the effects of which should be seen and felt to latest posterity."

In an odd twist to the story, the "Snow Ghost" has, through those generations, been blamed for a perceived profusion of snow that seems to accumulate on Sampson's Hill.

On the event of a snow storm, the Indian's ghost would magically redistribute massive mounds of snow on the hill, eternally vexing those who drove him to his death and any other mortals who dared to build on the hill. He would somehow make that snow deeper and heavier, and more difficult to shovel and plow.

"Thus," Buck wrote, "he would enjoy the satisfaction

of having them toil by day for what had been done in the night."

"Having lived in the vicinity of Sampson's Hill a quarter of a century," the author added, "I had long heard of this old tradition of the Indian ghost and his many marvelous freaks at piling up snow at the aforesaid places, which induced me to pay at least some attention to the matter.

"My observations have led me to confess that on the subsiding of a snow storm it is well worth anyone's going a mile to witness here its curious effects. Sometimes when but little more than an inch or two is left lying elsewhere on the hill, it would be seen heaped into hillocks of from four to ten feet high."

Ray Stahl, of the Upper Moreland Historical Society, takes both historical and personal interest in the old legend.

Stahl is active in historical affairs in Willow Grove and also resides on Sampson's Hill. "To this day," he said, "I see spots on that hill that seem to freeze sooner and stay frozen longer than in other areas. Regarding heavier snow–that's hard to tell."

Effie, and the Graveyard Ghost of Lower Merion

October, 1889. A mystery was about to unfold and a legend was about to be born.

Daylight was fading. Cloud shadows crawled across hillsides browned by autumn. On a quiet farm somewhere in the glens of Merion, a man was readying himself for a mission.

It was a nervous Joel Dull who mounted his faithful steed "Rosie" and set out on a date with the widow Effie Waters down in Merion Square.

As it turned out, it was Joel's date with destiny.

To reach Effie's, Joel and Rosie would have to pass the Lower Merion Baptist Church graveyard. And while it was Halloween eve, Joel had no fear. He was a staunch skeptic. He never gave ghosts a second thought.

Until that fateful night.

Joel was more ruffled about his meeting with Effie. He was not particularly experienced with women.

Effie's husband had fallen under the ice of the Schuylkill River and drowned the previous winter. Joel, who had known Effie before, allowed a fair mourning period to pass and finally got the nerve to ask if he could visit with the widow. She thought that would be nice.

And so, he trotted on Rosie toward what we now call Gladwyne and reached Effie's house just as night set in.

The moon and its celestial companions hung suspended in the sky in a night so clear these bodies seemed within arm's reach—as if they may be plucked from the vacuum void of the universe and placed in the pocket. Orion took aim at the Pleiades as they poked through the peak of the ever-blackening canopy.

Effie greeted Joel and instructed him to hitch Rosie to a post. She invited him in for conversation and some of her homemade wine.

Their smalltalk took a turn Joel could not have expected. But after all, it was only a few hours before the stroke of midnight and Halloween. So, Joel likely thought, why not talk *of ghosties and ghoulies and things that go bump in the night?*

But, Effie's colloquy might have been a bit uncomfortable for Joel. She spoke of the previous evening when the ghost of her husband visited her.

His arms were stretched toward her, as if pleading for help. His eyes were glazed over and in a fixed stare. After the fashion of his demise, he was soaking wet.

She told Joel that as she stood agape at the horrible sight, she attempted to speak to her beloved husband's specter. As her trembling words were uttered, however, the ghost vanished into thin air.

The story left Joel more than a little perplexed. He assured Effie that, with due respect to what she believed was her husband's spirit, there really was nothing to fear. Ghosts did not exist, he told her. It was all her imagination.

116

Her experience and his attitude must have caused a bit of uneasiness between them. She persevered, telling Joel of other eerie encounters, unexplainable sounds in her home, and her feeling that she was never really alone there.

With cautious cordiality, however, Joel and Effie chatted until nearly midnight.

Just before that hour, Joel unhitched Rosie and bade Effie farewell.

Into the night and through the deep woods the horse and rider proceeded.

All the talk of spooks and spirits–rejected, of course, by Joel–nonetheless had him on his guard. The night was clear and every turn of the road brought fresh shadows and new sounds.

Around one of those turns was the Lower Merion Baptist graveyard. And, as if sensing something from the other world, Rosie's canter slowed to a walk.

The horse rolled its head, whinnied, and became almost uncontrollable as Joel struggled with the reins.

As the tombstones of the graveyard came into view, Joel could not, as hard as he may have tried, purge his mind of the earlier conversation.

But, as he was certain there were *no such things as ghosts*, he would calm Rosie down and the two would make their way past the cemetery without incident.

From a distant hill, a church bell struck of first of twelve chimes. Halloween had come.

At once, a bone-chilling coldness wrapped Joel in its grip.

A cloud drifted in front of the moon. And, a rustling sound echoed from the graveyard.

Both rider and horse stood riveted in the roadway as from between the tombstones a dark, tall figure appeared.

His eyes widened and frozen with fear, his horse too frightened to move, Joel listened as the shadowy form spoke:

"Hark!" it said. "Hark! Your time has come!"

With that, Joel let out a shriek that spurred Rosie into a

gallop.

As the twelfth bell pealed from the distant church, the graveyard wraith disappeared into the darkness and Joel Dull simply disappeared.

Effie never saw Joel again.

In fact, Joel Dull seemed to have fallen off the face of the earth until he surfaced many years later.

A local chap told anyone who would listen that he had come across a bedraggled, confused, old man who had told him the details of this story and, between disordered and delirious babblings, claimed he was Joel Dull and every word he spoke was the frightful truth.

Folks in Lower Merion tended to scoff at the story. Surely, no ghost rose from in the graveyard. Surely, it was a watchman. Surely, the deranged old man had made the whole thing up.

Or...had he?

(The above story was adapted from several sources, including a 1979 article in the Main Line Times.)

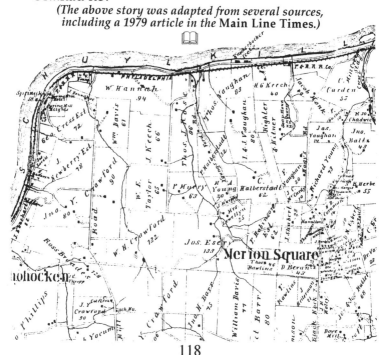

118

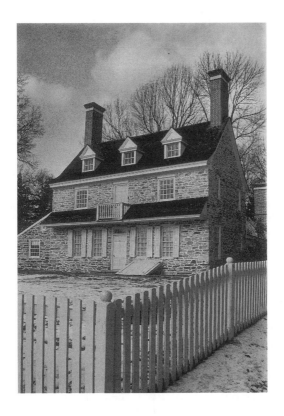

Harriton
Tuggie the Witch, and the Ghouls of Harriton

A few blocks from the hallowed halls of Bryn Mawr College, a few more blocks from the shops of Bryn Mawr borough, and smack dab in the middle of the luxurious Main Line enclave of Lower Merion Township is the place that gave that borough and that township those names.

It's Charles Thomson's old house.

Who's Charles Thomson?

George Washington received notice from Charles Thomson that he had been elected president. Benjamin Franklin called him friend.

Almost every day, every American can see and read something Charles Thomson left as a personal legacy.

This forgotten father of the United States was secretary of the Continental Congress during the Revolution, and his country estate still stands as one of the most pleasant surprises in Montgomery County.

By Main Line standards, the handsome home is considered "modest."

Million-dollar mansions now rise on the gently rolling hills which were once part of a 700-acre tract given by William Penn to Welsh Quaker Rowland Ellis in 1682. The "Welsh Tract" was settled quickly and the present home now known as Harriton was built in 1704.

The area was named Merion after Ellis' home of Merionethshire, Wales. The property itself was dubbed "Bryn Mawr," which is Welsh for "high hills."

In 1719, Maryland tobacco farmer Richard Harrison purchased the Ellis estate and renamed it Harriton. After Harrison's death, his daughter inherited the home and moved in with his new husband, Charles Thomson.

A native Irishman, Thomson was a scholar who tutored in classic Latin and Greek at the Academy, the forerunner of the University of Pennsylvania. He went on to establish himself as a peacemaker with the natives, a leader in the local Presbyterian church, and was a successful merchant.

As secretary of the Continental Congress, it was his name which attested the signing of the Declaration of Independence, and it was he who came up with the spread eagle and "E Pluribus Unum" symbols, which became the Great Seal of the United States.

Thomson was entrusted with the deepest secrets of the struggle for independence.

And today, his old home has secrets of its own.

MONTGOMERY COUNTY GHOST STORIES

It is the setting for a pair of stories which have been bent and shaped over the years, but remain as two of the county's most repeated legends.

They are the legends of Tuggie the witch and the Ghouls of Harriton–two quite distinct and different tales.

While the stories involve ghosts in a purely cursory manner, they are so much a part of local lore in Lower Merion that they warrant inclusion in this book.

But, as the details have been distorted as the legends have been whispered down the alley of time, both leave many unanswered questions and uncertain conclusions.

The legend is traced to the period of Richard Harrison's ownership of the house. In fact, it was shortly after Harrison, his family, and his slaves occupied the estate that Tuggie (also referred to as Tuggy in some accounts) committed a heinous act which backfired tragically.

In the slave quarters of Harriton, Tuggie was held in high esteem by some and feared by others. She was known to be the daughter of a powerful warrior and the niece of an African witch doctor. She had "the powers," it was said.

And among her fellow slaves, Tuggie was known to have within her the deepest hatred for her master, Richard Harrison. Not only taken as a slave from her village near the mouth of the Congo River, she was taken by Harrison from her family in Delaware.

A tragedy in the Harrison family provided the opportunity for Tuggie to take out her vengeance on her master.

One of Harrison's young daughters took ill and died. She was buried in the family graveyard on the grounds of Harriton.

As the story goes, an ancient tribal ritual dictated that revenge on a rival could be exacted at the time of the death of a member of that rival's family.

Three days after that death, Tuggie was taught, she should go to the daughter's grave and drive a stake through her heart.

121

This, she believed, would inflict a painful death on Richard Harrison.

But, Tuggie was taught that there was also a high risk. There was the real chance that the ghost of the deceased–in this case, the little girl–might rise from the grave and kill her.

Still another clause in this diabolical tradition told that the perpetrator of the reprisal could protect themself–in this case, Tuggie–by preparing a broth which would sicken and kill the targeted victim–in this case, Richard Harrison.

Tuggie took no chances. She laid out a plan to do both.

It seemed that every night before retiring, Harrison drank a cup of hot chocolate. That, Tuggie knew, would provide the opportunity she needed to complete one element of the plan.

She mixed the prescribed ingredients–the wart of a toad, parts of insects, the eye of a tomcat, a pinch of mold and graveyard soil, and others–and boiled it. As she prepared Master Harrison's cocoa, she blended a small amount into his nightcap.

Obligingly, as she had done so many other times before, she took the cup to his bedside.

And then, she slipped from the house and made her way through the bleak night to the graveyard.

With a mallet and a sharpened stake she had made earlier, she found the fresh grave of the little girl.

She knelt at the grave, positioned the stake carefully, raised the mallet, and with a fierce swing drove the razor-sharp rod into the loose dirt.

The stake pierced the soil and drove deeply, surely into the heart of the corpse.

Tuggie swelled with satisfaction.

But, as she tried to stand up, she was pulled down by an unseen force. She could not rise. Something was holding her down.

Again and again she tried to stand. Again and again, the force would not allow her to do so.

In a frantic flash, Tuggie realized what must have been

going on. The spirit of the little girl had materialized, grabbed her dress, and was pulling her into the grave. Her plan had failed. She was to die at the hand of a ghost!

With that, Tuggie let out a blood-curdling scream that echoed from the graveyard to the Harriton House.

Richard Harrison, who had at that very instant raised his cup of cocoa to his mouth, was rattled by the hellish shriek. It shook him so that he spilled the witches' brew-laced drink to the floor.

Harrison gathered household members to see from where and whom the scream emanated. Under the faint light of a waning moon they made their way to the burial ground.

There, by the little girl's grave, was Tuggie.

She lay face up, her eyes as big as quarters, fixed in eternal fear. Her mouth was wide open, frozen in that final outcry.

Tuggie was dead.

And, as the search party looked more closely, they noticed something that only a few of the slaves would know the significance of. Her dress was wedged firmly into the ground by a stake!

Tuggie's body was taken back to the slave quarters by her compatriots, and a confused Richard Harrison returned to his mansion.

As he walked into his bedchamber, he noticed that his cat was lapping up the spilled cocoa.

He dismissed that, and turned to his wardrobe to dress for bed.

When he turned back toward his bed, he looked again and saw the cat.

It was still next to the spilled cocoa.

It was dead.

And, it has been said that Tuggie's restless ghost still can be seen wandering around the Harriton property—eyes and mouth still open wide in a perpetual panic.

———◆———

As for the Ghouls of Harriton, most of that legend has

been completely muddled by time.

The "ghouls" were a band of rogues who, in the 19th century, were to have taken the remains of Charles Thomson from his grave in the Harriton burial ground.

The keepers of the flames of lore and legend in Lower Merion contend that if those graverobbers ever really existed, they failed in their attempt to steal Thomson's body. And, if any grave really was ever robbed, it was likely that of a slave.

But, who knows? Perhaps the Ghouls of Harriton may have been chased away by the *Ghost* of Harriton–Tuggie.

Stranger things have happened!

The Little Lady in Gray,
The Phantom Hitch-Hiker
and Other Main Line Ghosts

There once was a marvelous mansion on Montgomery Avenue where the dalliances of a pair of Civil War-era spirits became so frequent and so frightening that serious researchers came to investigate and validate their presences.

What their probe uncovered launched one of the most sensational ghost stories of late 19th and early 20th century Montgomery County.

Up until the time the old McGeorge house was demolished in 1934, family members continued to honor the oft-told tale of "The Colonel" and "The Little Lady in Gray."

The house was built just before the Civil War and occupied by the McGeorge family in 1883. Over the years the McGeorges resided there, generation after generation claimed to have seen the mysterious couple glide through the house and show up just about anywhere, at any time.

Described as wearing a Civil War-era gown and a shawl fastened with a brooch, the "Little Lady" could most often be seen passing down a staircase, a hallway, and taking a seat in the library. When someone stared at her or spoke to her, she would vanish.

Her ghost was often accompanied by the faint sound of her rustling gown.

And, she could sometimes be seen in the company of the second entity of the McGeorge house, "The Colonel."

Clad in the dress uniform of a Union colonel, the male spirit would also appear with a certain audible fanfare–a rattling saber.

And, when both the rustling gown and rattling saber were heard in close proximity, which did happen on occasion, it was assumed by those who witnessed it that the two might somehow have been more than strangers while they were alive.

It was not unusual, according to stories passed down through the years, to see the Colonel and the Little Lady together in wraithy rendezvous by the parlor hearth.

Further, if the Colonel chose not to haunt that hearth when the Little Lady came to call, she would play sad music on the nearby grand piano.

So many credible family members and interested visitors heard the sounds, saw the forms, and felt the presences that folks in the neighborhood were fairly convinced that something odd was going on in the McGeorge house.

Theories abounded. The Little Lady was a spurned woman who lived as an "old maid" and died peacefully in the house. Or, she was murdered there–and her skeleton was boarded up inside a wall.

The Colonel committed suicide, for whatever reason, in the house. Their stories were never truly uncovered.

While their earthly existences remained a mystery, their unearthly visitations became a part of the darker side of Lower Merion's history.

In the years between the time its last tenants moved out and its demolition, the McGeorge place became the local "haunted house." Boarded up and eerie, the mansion was finally cleared to make room for the apartment complexes that stand on its site today.

Does the Colonel's saber still rattle there? Can the rustling sound of a gown be heard? How about a faint, melancholy melody from a phantom piano?

Only those who reside on what was the old McGeorge estate can say.

Skipping on and off the Main Line, many more tantalizing tales emerge from old documents, scrapbooks, and newspaper accounts.

They are tantalizing mostly because of the scant details that remain.

Still, while the thread is thin, it is strong enough to keep

126

these stories woven into the fiber of Montgomery County's heritage.

Take, for example, the "Hitch-Hiking Ghost" of Westminster Cemetery.

Founded in 1884, Westminster is tucked into the extreme corner of Montgomery County, just over the Philadelphia city line and perched on rolling hills as high as 275 feet above the Schuylkill River.

When we visited Westminster, no one there had heard of the story. But, a secretary did tell us a story that lingers in the history of that corner of Lower Merion Township.

The story dates to when the cemetery was rural and remote, and a train station, Barmouth, was built there specifically to accommodate mourners.

It was at that station where a man was murdered, and his killer was never found, we were told.

That story seems to have no relationship, however, to the ghostly hitch-hiker of Westminster.

And, anyone familiar with popular "urban legends" may snub their nose at the "hitch-hiking ghost" of Westminster Cemetery.

It goes something like this: When the moon is particularly bright, the ghost of a young woman supposedly wanders through Westminster. Should a motorist pass by, the ghostly–but quite "normal"-looking girl thumbs a lift.

If picked up, she asks for a ride back to her home in Germantown. And, if taken there, the "normal"-looking woman thanks her benefactor, gets out of the car, and vanishes in the night.

In 1934, the ghost story created such a stir that local police were called to the cemetery to disburse a large gathering that had gone there on reports that the ghost had been sighted.

It was, as best as we could determine, the last sighting of the hitch-hiking ghost.

Probing through stacks of old newspaper articles, scrapbooks, and documents, some fragments of ghost stories–most little more than a seductive sentence or two–

open up all kinds of possibilities.

The famous "Overhanging Rock" which juts into Route 320 at Gulph Mills is one of the most unusual historical landmarks in the nation.

The Hanging Rock at Gulph Mills near Conshohocken, Pa.

At, under, and around it, the Continental Army camped from December 13 to December 19, 1777. It was the last encampment before settling in for the winter at Valley Forge.

When the rock, and the land upon which it is situated, was given to the Valley Forge Historical Society in 1924, society vice-president J. Aubrey Anderson accepted, and said: "No man-made monument can surpass its beauty, or equal its power to arrest attention and fire the imagination. It is unique. It is impressive. It is one of nature's wonders."

While portions of the rock have been chipped away to accommodate the state highway, the rock has remained largely intact due to pressure put upon the highway department by historians and preservationists.

Today, as traffic whizzes past the rock, it follows the

same path that the brave soldiers of Washington's army took during that cold, hard winter.

And, while any ghost at the Overhanging Rock might presumably be that of one of those soldiers, it is not.

And, in fact, it cannot be determined exactly who it–she–may be.

She is one of those enigmatic snippets of a ghost who popped up in one reference and seemed to disappear from the ledgers after that.

What is known is that the ghostly form of a lovely young woman with long, flowing hair has been seen gliding on the roadway at the Overhanging Rock.

And when conditions are right, the long-haired ghost can also be heard moaning in the night.

At the other end of the Upper and Lower Merion Townships southeastern "panhandle" of Montgomery County is Penn Valley, a well-developed area which once abounded with mysteries, legends, and ghosts.

Even the most keen of historians down that way were unsure of the locations and/or origins of certain ominous and archaic place names–Bowlers Woods, Murder Orchard among them–but each of these esoteric locales were settings for the legends of Penn Valley so long ago.

Centennial Road today winds over hill and dale and is lined with premium palaces of suburbia. Who knows, though, if any of those who reside on those lovely properties may still feel the presences that once permeated that area?

One ghost which made itself quite conspicuous in the early 1900s was that of William Crossley.

It was in July, 1905 when Crossley, a Germantown clockmaker, was heading home from Narberth when he stopped for a drink of cool water at a spring on the Augustus Hoehler farm.

The Hoehler family was at work in their fields when the repeat of two shots rang through the woods.

The Hoehlers scurried toward the source of the gunshots and found the body of William Crossley by the spring. He was shot twice in the mouth.

They turned their attention quickly to the nearby trees, where they caught a glimpse of two men running frantically into the depths of the forest.

The county coroner, and then a coroner's jury, ruled his death a suicide, although the local police disagreed. They discovered that Crossley's repair bag was empty (indicating a robbery) and–a fact that somehow, and incredibly, must have eluded the coroner–there was no pistol by the dead man's side (indicating murder).

For many years, it was said that the clockmaker's ghost could be seen and heard, walking and whining along Centennial Road, seeking anyone who would pause a while so he could tell them the real story of his tragic death that day.

Ghost stories were told by the old-timers of the early 20th century, set in places such as Bowlers Woods (where eerie, glowing forms would be seen and frightening moans and screams would be heard) and Murder Orchard (where could be seen the ghost of a man who had hanged himself from one of the orchard trees).

These days, Bowlers Woods, which was named after an early property owner, is part of Gulley Run Park. And, Murder Orchard was in an area now roughly bordered by Cleveland, Brookhurst, and S. Woodbine Aves.

But of all these pitifully incomplete and powerfully appealing stories, a story which screams out to the author for more intensive research, it is the story of one ghost which, at one time, haunted the Beechwood Road area of Penn Wynne.

Not even modicum of detail of the origin of this particular spirit has been left to tease the imagination– but one quite tantalizing morsel has.

This ghost was reported by whomever, whenever, to wander that place totally nude.

Should anyone ever, *ever* spot this spirit, contact the authors immediately. An investigation is promised!

📖

MONTGOMERY COUNTY GHOST STORIES

The Montgomery County Ghost Chronicles

As our census of Montgomery County's ghostly population proceeded, we counted several stories which provided only minimal details.

In some cases, time has washed away the who, what, or when of the accounts. In others–in what we call *"they say"* stories–the *"they"* could never be determined and the stories suffered in their sketchy specifics.

This chapter will serve as a "catch-all" of those stories. A review, if you will, of those tales that do not warrant sections unto themselves, but are important enough to include in this volume.

We will begin at a private club on a hillside in **Glenside** where reports of a ghost have sparked costume galas at Halloween and much discussion among members and visitors alike.

Many jovial nights and splendid special events have played out at the **North Penn VFW Post 676** .

Its loyal membership has created a lively post, and the building's past and position on Jenkintown Road have contributed to more than one mystery there.

One is believed to be traceable to December 7, 1777, when the "Battle of Edge Hill" raged briefly but fiercely at nearby Whitemarsh.

More a skirmish than a "battle," Edge Hill nonetheless cost the lives of an estimated 40 British soldiers and a like number of Americans.

The bodies of the Americans were buried in a wooded area along Edge Hill Road. As development crept into the area, the scant remains of four of them were discovered, removed, and reinterred on the grounds of Post 676.

It is from these graves, prominently marked and memorialized at the post entrance, that the spirit energy is believed to emanate.

Workers at the post have reported the sounds of footsteps and chair-dragging on the floor of the banquet room long after the last human occupant had departed.

Photographic evidence of a ghost at the North Penn VFW?

One bartender said he often spies, in a fleeting glimpse, a shadowy form pass by. And, two photographs taken by separate individuals at separate times, seem to clearly depict apparitional anomalies. The pictures are on display behind the post bar.

The notion that VFW Post 676 is haunted has become so intriguing and inviting that the Glenside facility has hosted several highly successful Halloween parties and dances at which the curious may mingle with the building's resident wraiths.

📖

Near the Hope Lodge and Mather Mill, where Route 73 and the Bethlehem Pike cross in **Ft. Washington**, is the **Bent Elbo** at Fortside, a popular restaurant and banquet hall.

The present structure was built in 1883 on the site of a previous inn and private residence.

Considering its prominent position at the intersection of two of the county's earliest and busiest roads, much history has passed its way.

And, while George Washington may have dropped by...while the Liberty Bell scurried past on its way to safekeeping upstate...and while local lore has it that Princess Grace Kelly had her first alcoholic beverage there...it is better known for the purposes of this book as a haunted inn.

By whom it is haunted, and the intensity of the energy are still unanswered questions, however.

What is known is that several customers and staffers have reported "odd sensations" there, and at least one doorman, after saying he saw a shadowy figure in the basement, has said there is "something" down there.

"I haven't seen anything myself," said Mark Rohlfing, owner of the Bent Elbo.

"But, I have seen band members who had been changing upstairs come down with strange stories. One guy had been brushing his teeth. When he came down his face was as white as the toothpaste. He said he had seen *something* up there."

📖

MONTGOMERY COUNTY GHOST STORIES

It would take a fertile imagination to transport the 21st century mind back several hundred years to when the Fraizers Hill section of **Willow Grove** was a desolate, mysterious place where crops were bountiful, the forests were thick, and a handful of intrepid settlers huddled in tiny cabins and shacks.

It was known as Horseheaven then–and it was a place where legends grew as tall as the chestnut trees.

Its very name conjures up bizarre images. Political boundaries have, over the centuries, divided the region into the towns and townships we now know.

That one ridge, however, was so treacherous for early stagecoaches that many horses lost their footing, fell, and died there. The locals came to call it "Horse Heaven."

According to one legend, that was quickly contracted into "Horseheaven," and eventually was completely corrupted to its modern descendant–Horsham.

One of those old stories of that hill still resounds in the folklore of the area–the legend of great giant of Horseheaven.

For the story, we turn once more to historian William J. Buck, who included the story in his *Local Sketches and Legends* in 1887.

Buck was quite assertive in his assessment of the "giant" story and other tales of creatures and ghosts that once roamed the Willow Grove area.

He mentioned Washington Irving's *Rip Van Winkle* and *Legend of Sleepy Hollow* classics and wrote, "I am inclined to believe that for variety of incident traditions of this hill surpass either."

With that lofty appraisal, Buck wrote of what he described as "...the giant spectre that took his walks across the bleak surface of the hill from one woods to the other, chiefly in the nights of autumn and winter, but at nearly all hours."

Does that spectre still stroll in the night on that hill–among the very ghosts of its old woods? William Buck was firm on that: "I will predict that," he said in his 1887 writing, "the spectre will not forsake his old accustomed haunts."

And, if it still does ramble Fraizers Hill, it would be wise to give it a wide berth!

Buck noted that the beast was "Occasionally from ten to fifteen feet in height, of a dark brown color and accompanied by a fearful rustling din.

"Sometimes going at a moderate walk but frequently at an increasing speed, as if belated and determined to accomplish his mission or round within a given time," he added.

The creature made no attempt to hide. Through thickets and fields alike it strode. "A perfect calm with ordinary darkness appeared to suit him best to be abroad with his unfailing accompaniment of detestable noise," Buck continued.

"It mattered not whether it was but one, two, three, or more persons together, for the spectre had no dread of numbers, and they could all behold him.

"Sometimes it proceeded onwards fifty or one hundred yards in advance; on other occasions following, or now and then making a sudden turn to the right or left, and finally disappearing in the darkness without it being known to offer harm to anyone."

It must be noted that in his chapter, "Traditions and Wonders of Horseheaven," Buck offered certain possible explanations and rationalizations for the giant spectre. But, for the purposes of this book, in this time, we shall stop short of repeating them.

We will, however, say that Buck, who claimed that on two occasions he, himself, had seen the giant, closed his chapter with prophetic thoughts.

As he mused on the many legends, creatures, and ghosts that roamed (and, likely, *still* roam) across "Horseheaven," he wrote:

"Though I may soon pass away and be forgotten, let the memories of this hill survive, yes, let them be cherished and my object herein will be accomplished."

MONTGOMERY COUNTY GHOST STORIES

Those memories, dear Mr. Buck, have survived. And you are to be praised for passing them along so that we, too, may share them with more generations in Lower Moreland, Montgomery County, and beyond.

📖

Along the banks of the **Unami Creek** as it flows into the Perkiomen Creek in **Marlborough Township**, ghost stories have circulated since the turn of the 19th century.

They centered around the old mills that drew their power from upstream near Sumneytown.

Those mills included Jacob Dasch's gunpowder mill which was built in 1780. Dasch (also mentioned in some documents as *Dast*) met an unfortunate fate when his mill exploded and he was killed.

These were crude mills, obviously, and over the nearly 80 years of their existence along the Unami, Dasch's was but one of five dozen fatalities which have been documented by historians.

Any one of those victims could be the baseline of the hauntings along the Unami. Many individuals throughout the years have reported seeing one of two spirits which are said to reside in the area of the old powder mills.

One carries a lantern and can be seen swaying that lantern as it strolls along the creek. When noticed by a passerby, the ghost extinguishes its light, appears for an instant as a shadowy silhouette, and then vanishes.

The other apparition is a headless form that pushes a wheelbarrow silently through whatever contemporary barriers it may face.

📖

A popular tale of more recent vintage is that of a ghostly hitch-hiker who appears from time to time on **Route 202 just north of Norristown**.

She has come to be known as "Lucy," and is said to have been the victim of a car accident several years ago on the spot where she now appears.

Lucy seems as "human" as any other living being as

136

she thumbs or flags down her ride.

But, as the benevolent motorist coasts past her to pull safely off to the side of the road, Lucy is nowhere to be seen.

📖

As nebulous as "Lucy" is a ghost recorded in history only as an anonymous Indian who prowls the **Swamp Creek**, apparently not far from another Indian whose spirit wanders the ridge at Sunrise Mill.

This particular entity reportedly resided alone around 1780 and did odd jobs for local farmers.

The story goes that a peddler who was passing through the area disappeared, and the old Indian retreated to his humble home at about the same time. He no longer offered his services to the farmers and mysteriously kept to himself.

Although the folks in the area fully suspected that the peddler had been murdered and the Indian was the murderer, the Indian was never formally charged.

The peddler was never again seen, but the Indian was eventually found dead in his cabin.

And, it wasn't long until reports started to surface that the Indian's ghost could be spotted occasionally around **Leidy's Graveyard**.

The ghost has been described as silent but swift as it glides through field and forest, and all who have seen it say it is pure, glistening white in appearance.

It materializes for only a brief moment and vanishes as unannounced as it arrived.

📖

Montgomery County is not without its own "monster" legend, *a la* "Bigfoot" or "Sasquatch."

Here, it has surfaced every few decades to torment folks around northwestern Montgomery and neighboring Chester and Berks counties.

In February, 1932, papers in West Chester and Coatesville bristled with reports of strange tracks in the snow and stranger sightings of a bizarre beast. The papers went so far as to link the incident with the "Jersey Devil" legend of the Garden State.

Thirteen years later, a shrieking, leaping creature was sighted in North Coventry Township and Pottstown. Again, it was identified as the "Jersey Devil."

In March, 1973, another wave of real or imagined hysteria swept Pottstown and environs as what was described as a tall, winged, reddish-black, cat-like creature with red eyes, long, sharp claws, and a tail ravaged its way through chicken coops as it took bounds of up to 20 feet through farms around the borough.

The sightings–and the shredded poultry–created a wild disturbance, wilder searches, and even wilder stories as it became known as the **"Pottstown Monster"** before fading into the files of Montgomery County's urban legends.

📖

There are so many more stories that could have been added to these ghost chronicles of Montgomery County.

Some, such as in restaurants or business places in Trappe, Pottstown, Royersford, and Harleysville never made it to these pages because their proprietors opted against what they might have considered "bad publicity."

Other old tales, such as the accounts of how demons would appear in a burst of sulphur on the old Medlock Farm on the Skippack Pike near **Center Square**, or the 1920 poltergeist activity on Forest Avenue in **Ambler**, could not be elaborated on because their sources could not be traced to our satisfaction.

We received a long letter from a writer who claimed to have had an encounter at the **Kennedy Mansion** (a National Park Service-owned building in which a restaurant was located at the time this book was written).

The correspondent said a "transparent, but sort of cloudy figure of a man" appeared in a window of the mansion when it lay fallow for many years before its restoration.

But alas, that writer provided no return address, so

further details could not be secured.

📖

We tried several times to ascertain if anyone in what was the old Crossroads Hotel along **Neiffer Road** in Limerick Township has seen the ghost of a Colonial soldier lately, but failed in those attempts.

📖

Has the ghostly image of an elderly woman really been seen relaxing on a rocking chair in **Boland Hall**, on the Montgomery County side of **St. Joseph's University** campus? Are disembodied footsteps and the echoing sound of a bell still heard there? Although we received such reports from reliable sources, we could not confirm those incidents.

📖

The charming old blacksmith's house of the former Walnut Grove Farm in **Gulph Mills** now serves as the home of the superintendent of the Gulph Mills Golf Club. A newspaper article ferreted from the files of the Upper Merion Township Library mentioned an old story about a distraught woman who hanged herself in the house and how her ghost was suspected as haunting it.

Yes, there are so many more places we did not have time to investigate–so many more stories left to be told.

Perhaps, at another time, in another book, we shall.

📖

Several ghosts roam the roads, shops, and restaurants of Skippack Village.

Skippack Spooks

Throughout the year, countless thousands of people pour into the shops and restaurants of Skippack Village, along Route 73 in Skippack Township.

What most of them don't know is that among them are several ghosts that share those shops and restaurants and occasionally make life interesting for those who work in those places.

At the Road House Grille on Mensch Road, several indicators have led several employees to firmly believe that the superb restaurant is haunted.

Damon Giangreco, the restaurant manager who professes to be a firm non-believer in ghosts, does concede that unusual things have happened, even to him.

"Every night," he said, "we clean up every dining room. One time we came in the next morning and around that plant [pointing to a potted plant in the bar area] there was silverware and glasses set all around its base.

"Now," he continued, "I check everything before I leave. It was definitely not like that when I left the previous night."

In recent years, the faint scents of baby powder or perfume have wafted through parts of the restaurant where no such aromas should be detected. Banging sounds, crunching noises–all easily distinguishable from the expected sounds of a restaurant–have also caught the attention of those who work within the walls of the Road House.

"We hear things late at night," according to Michael Suminski, executive chef at the Road House. "It's like a dropping sound. And there's that time I was going back toward the kitchen and out of the corner of my eye I saw a man sitting at the end of the bar. He was wearing a black suit and a black hat. I turned around before I got to the kitchen door because I thought that maybe he wasn't getting waited on.

"I came back, and there was nobody there. I started to think about it more, and everything I saw had been crystal clear–except for his face. That was very fuzzy, no detail."

Suminski said the odd occurrences have not been limited to the hours of night.

"Just the other day," he continued, "I was the first person here. It was dark and quiet, about ten of eleven in the morning. I locked the door behind me and the back door was still locked. I let our server, Joanne, in at about eleven and locked the door behind her because we weren't open yet.

"I started upstairs and I heard the stereo go on upstairs. Then, I heard the office door close!"

The chef said there were no open window, nothing to create a draft strong enough to close that door.

"I called for Joanne and she came up to the landing. Then, we both heard the door open and close again. It was a very distinct sound.

"It freaked us out enough that we both went around the building looking for someone who might have been in the

141

place. There was, of course, no one."

A bit of information about the history of the building could add an interesting twist to the mysterious opening and closing of that door.

Before the building became a restaurant, it was a funeral parlor. And, before the room behind that door became an office, it was a viewing room.

While Michael Suminski and others might get "freaked out" by things that happen at the Road House, they are never purely frightened. In fact, Suminski, is upbeat about the whole matter.

"There's never a bad feeling," he mused, "nothing negative. And hey, if I was a ghost? I wouldn't mind being trapped in a bar!"

📖

Just down the Skippack Pike a short distance from the Road House is another eatery with its own set of mysteries.

Mal's American Diner is a "down home" kind of place where, among other things, the waitstaff has witnessed sugar packets moving on their own, the radio and lights turning themselves on, and phantom footsteps that can be heard on occasion on the steps to the basement.

At Mal's, James Fulton told of one incident that still mystifies him.

"I was driving past one night. I saw that a light was on. I stopped in. And, as I was coming into the back room to make sure that the back door was locked, I saw a shadow running underneath a table."

Fulton couldn't explain it further. It was, simply, a shadowy form that slithered under the tables. He can tell us what he did after seeing it–he turned around and bolted out of the place! "I was spooked," he nodded.

Sue Buckwalter, a waitress and cook at Mal's, truly believes there is a presence or two in the building which was once a service station. She further believes, as do some neighbors, that the ghosts are those of previous owners of the property.

Sue told us of her own experiences at Mal's.

"It was really early in the morning when most of the weird stuff would happen. I went to make coffee and, as the coffee was dripping down into the pot, the coffee basket actually flew out of the coffee machine and hit the counter about six or seven feet away. Nobody had touched it, nobody was anywhere near it. And, several customers witnessed it."

Trisa Ziegler, a former waitress, offered an incident that she experienced at the other end of the business day. It convinced her that there is an entity in the eatery.

"One night, we were closing. There were four of us sitting around. There was a broom propped up against the ice machine.

"The ghost picked the broom up. It went up in mid-air and flied into the foyer. We just sat there and watched it happen. Then, we just left...quickly!"

One specialty shop owner in the village had yet another story to tell, but she asked that we not use her name or mention her shop. "I'm really not sure I even am comfortable with any ghost stories being mentioned in Skippack," she said. "Maybe it would be bad for business."

No, ma'am, not the case. After penning books in such tourist meccas as Cape May and the Pocono Mountains, it has been our experience that a good ghost story or two seems to actually bring people in for a possible look-see of their own. And, a strong foundation of folklore any village or town such as Skippack adds character.

It was still with some hesitation–but with a convincing demeanor–that the woman told us her story. The words are hers, as transcribed from a taped interview.

"I can't call myself a believer in any of this ghost stuff," she said. "But, I've heard enough, read enough, and seen enough movies about the subject that I can't discount the possibility that there is something out there, somewhere.

"And, what happened to me one day here almost validated it all and made me a believer. But, I'm still not convinced.

"There's not a whole lot to it, but I can tell you that I was coming out of my shop–out of the side door which we use after hours–and I had closed things down. There was no doubt, I had turned the lights off, all the spigots were closed, and there was positively no one inside. It's a small shop, and no one could hide anywhere there without being noticed.

"Well, I came out the side door toward my car and, as I had a thousand times, locked the door behind me. As I locked and checked the door handle, it was almost as if I had hit the switch that turned on the ghost.

"Two lights in our front window clicked on. I heard the radio playing. I thought, OK, when I pulled the door shut, I made enough vibration for all of that to happen. But the real me knew that wasn't possible.

"I didn't know what to do at first. Should I go in and check? Would that be stupid? Well, sometimes I'm kind of stupid, I guess, so I went back in.

"And, this I swear to you. As I took my first step inside, the lights and the radio went off. And then, it got really weird.

"Of course, the radio and lights going off caught my attention. I looked up, and as I glanced toward the sales counter, I saw what I have read so many people describe–a glowing form or figure.

"I couldn't really tell if it was in front of, behind, or *in* the counter. I just know that, as they said in *Camelot*, 'for one, brief, shining moment' I saw something–something that looked like a filmy or smoky, and slightly luminous–being standing there.

"I just stared blindly for those few seconds, not knowing what would happen next.

"Well, nothing did. I must have stood there, frozen in my place, for a good five minutes, my eyes darting around

144

looking and waiting. And, nothing happened.

"Needless to say, when I finally got up the nerve to leave–after making a thorough check of all electrical outlets, switches, and whatnot–I didn't know what to expect.

"But, I locked the door, jiggled the handle, and slowly backed away toward my car. To make a long story short, nothing happened.

"I'll never be able to explain it. I have told maybe five people about it, and they can't explain it, either.

"Was it a ghost? Was it some electrical thingie? I don't know.

"Would I like to know? I guess. But, then again, maybe I wouldn't. Every once in awhile, though, when things are quiet in the shop, I wait for something else to happen.

"If it does, maybe I'd be a believer in all of this. Until then, though, I'm still on the fence."

Skippack Village

The desecrated former Hood family crypt.

The Body Snatchers of Limerick

The car crept down Possum Hollow Road, the gravel of the lane crunching beneath the tires as they rolled slowly on what could be the quintessential gateway to ghost hunting.

There was a time when stage coaches, carriages,

trolleys and canal boats traversed what is now scrubland wedged between a nuclear power plant and a superhighway.

This is where George Washington passed by as he maneuvered his troops into position, and where "Mad Anthony" Wayne led his men on a daring crossing of the Schuylkill River in 1777.

It is where highwaymen found easy prey on those passing coaches. Where gypsies set up camp and told fortunes in the forest. Where boatsmen, shad fishermen, and farmers often squabbled.

In this quiet corner of Limerick Township, there are now but ruins and ravaged reminders of those storied times.

Along Possum Hollow Road, it *looks* like a good place for a haunting. And, it *is* such a place.

It is a place of a genuine ghoulish act very long ago...of ghastly misdeeds and misconceptions...and of some very real ghost stories.

On that gloomy winter's morning, we approached our destination with caution. As the stacks of the Limerick generating station belched steam into the steel-gray sky, we found the tomb, and then the manor house, that are forever inscribed in the ledgers of lore in Limerick.

The research team—investigators Debbi Kerr, Kimberly Pikunis and this author—followed directions given to us by a seasoned citizen in a Limerick restaurant and came upon our destination with relative ease.

But, the story about what happened there is somewhat uneasy to imagine.

We groped our way down a leaf-matted embankment toward the slender stream known as Possum Hollow Run.

About halfway between road and rivulet, we spotted the distinctive rocky crown of the Hood family tomb.

It is an eerie sight. Once, it stood serene and sacred on that embankment, facing the family mansion which rose on the next hill. Once, it held within the remains of John McClellan Hood, his wife, and their children.

147

MONTGOMERY COUNTY GHOST STORIES

Once, an obelisk monument marked the spot. Today, a tangled underbrush strangles the stone sepulcher. Considering for what purpose it was erected and what it looks like now, it is a depressing place.

The monument paid tribute to the Hood family luminary, Captain Washington Hood.

The son of Irish immigrant John McClellan Hood and his German-born wife, Elizabeth Forebaugh, Washington Hood was born in 1808 and earned an appointment to the United States Military Academy.

After his studies at West Point (where, incidentally, he was the 500th graduate), Second Lieutenant Washington Hood was assigned to cartographic expeditions on the American frontiers.

He made his mark as the leader of the team that created the first formal maps of territories west of the Mississippi River.

Hood died in 1840 and his body was returned to his family home in Limerick Township. He was to "rest in peace" in the family crypt along Possum Hollow Road.

But, as you will read, that peaceful rest was rudely interrupted.

No one is certain exactly when it happened, but sometime in the early 20th century, the sepulcher was savagely and senselessly desecrated by persons unknown.

Hood family caskets were split open. Bones were stolen or scattered on the creekside. What was left of the corpses was left for curious ghouls to gawk over. The family tomb, which should have been sacrosanct, was vandalized, violated, and blasphemed.

The tomb, set in a dreary dale reminiscent of one generation's *Sleepy Hollow* and another's *Blair Witch Project*, quickly became the local "haunted" spot.

Ghosts, no doubt the quite angry ghosts of the Hood family members, were said to ramble freely in that dale. Glowing forms and rattling sounds were reported often by those who ventured to the old crypt.

The intensity of the insanity came to a head in the

summer of 1962 when the ghostly activity drew the attention of the local media and the local barracks of the Pennsylvania State Police.

Some teenagers with rather fertile imaginations stirred up quite a fuss when they reported mysterious noises down by the Hood crypt.

Soon enough, dozens of cars wound down Possum Hollow Road in search of the ghosts. State troopers responded and investigated.

That probe turned up what are two of the banes of the serious researcher of the supernatural–pranksters and Mother Nature. Crude cowbells were strung in trees by unknown mortals to create the "clanging" sounds. The "glowing forms" were deemed to be nothing more than phosphorous discharges from rotting logs and leaves.

The Great Possum Hollow Ghost Hunt of 1962 turned out to be a great hoax.

But, do ghosts really haunt the old Hood place?

To seek an answer to that question, we ventured forth along Possum Hollow Road and found Bessy Bell Farm, the Hood family homestead on–and please note this–*private property* not far from the old crypt.

Bessy Bell

After explaining our quest to a congenial tenant in the circa-1834 stone mansion, we were invited in for a look at a true historical and architectural gem of a building.

John McC. Hood came to the United States from Newtownstewart, County Tyrone, in the present Northern Ireland. He fashioned his Pennsylvania home after a manor house in that market town by the River Mourne.

While the Montgomery County Bessy Bell stands in the shadow of the cooling towers of a nuclear plant, the backdrop of that original Irish manor house were the curiously-named twin peaks of Bessy Bell and Mary Gray. Hood chose to call his new farm Bessy Bell. According to officials in Newtownstewart, N.I., the names of the hills there came from the daughters of a Scottish farmer who was among the first to settle that area.

The day we happened to visit Bessy Bell was well-suited for spirit searching. With all the attributes of a weathered Irish manor house, the mansion was wrapped in a soft mist and framed by twisted trees as it came into view along the rutted road that is its driveway.

It should be the mansion of the wealthy. It should be a stately bed and breakfast. It should stand proud and protected. Rather, it stands on the brink of extinction.

There are those who would demolish it in favor of more profitable pursuits. There are those who would preserve it as the centerpiece of a golf course. And then, there was the tenant we met who was laboriously stabilizing and refurbishing the place one room at a time.

Just outside the garden door of the mansion is the old obelisk that once stood at the crypt. It is believed that the remains of five Hood family members are buried somewhere in the soil of the yard.

There are many mysteries at Bessy Bell (a.k.a. Bessybell). Are the portals and arches in the basement remnants of tunnels and vaults where runaway slaves were secreted along the "Underground Railroad?" Or, are they merely architectural features?

As for ghosts, the most recent tenant knew of none and

has sensed nothing.

And although Bessy Bell and the lands surrounding it seem to be quite hospitable to spirit activity, no substantive stories have been told there.

We spoke with noted area historian Betty Wlazelek, who could recall nothing–other than the lurid events at the Hood crypt–of a ghostly nature.

This is not to say, however, that this magnificent old manor house may indeed harbor a spook or two.

Only time will tell if, someday, they will rise and be recognized.

It is believed that several Hood family members' remains are buried near this monument, relocated from the family's desecrated crypt.

Grey Towers Castle, Beaver College
Haunted Halls of Higher Learning

I: The Ghosts of Grey Towers

Montgomery County is blessed with some of the finest colleges and universities in the United States.

Their campuses are among the most picturesque and historic in the country, and their educational opportunities consistently place them in the very highest ranks of American institutes of higher learning.

And, within the walls of their stately buildings or on their quadrangles and campuses are also some of the most intriguing mysteries in all academia.

In this chapter we shall visit three superb colleges that are well within the county's borders, and another which straddles the Montgomery/Delaware county line. And, we shall meet the ghosts of those who walk among the living there.

Let us first turn off the busy roadways of Glenside and pass through the gates into the 55 tranquil acres that make up the campus of Beaver College.

MONTGOMERY COUNTY GHOST STORIES

Consistently rated high for its educational value and academic *values*, Beaver College is also well known for its ghosts.

The college's history is fascinating.

Founded as a frontier school for women in Beaver, western Pennsylvania, in 1853, it became a college in 1872.

In 1925, the college moved east to Jenkintown. Three years later, the main campus moved to its present site while a branch campus was maintained in Jenkintown. In 1962, operations were consolidated in the Glenside campus.

Since 1929, the central building on the Beaver College campus has been Grey Towers.

Inspired by Alnwick (pronounced Annick) Castle in Northumberland, England, Grey Towers is a National Historic Landmark and a truly remarkable architectural and artistic gem.

It was William Welsh Harrison, whose family owned the Franklin Sugar Refinery, who hired noted architect Horace Trumbauer to design a grand home on his estate.

The result is Grey Towers.

The 40-room home was, in its day, one of the largest private residences in the nation.

The details of its ornaments, elements, appointments and appurtenances are available at the college or on its internet site. Suffice to say it is, well, eclectic and eccentric.

There are few, if any, more important or impressive "Old Mains" on any colleges anywhere in this country.

And, few with ghost stories as interesting as the ghost stories handed down by generations of Beaver College students.

So well known are these stories that the college actually posted an account on its official web site. As part of the centenary of what it calls "The Castle" in 1998, throngs attended a "Haunted Castle" event there.

The ghost stories–to the chagrin of some folks at the college–just won't go away.

What's more, they were perpetuated on a video documentary, *College Hauntings*, produced in 1998 by noted videographer Gary White.

White found the perfect setting for his project. With its gaping, gurgling gargoyles, eerie angles, and lavish interior, Grey Towers could have been a set of a Hollywood thriller.

But, it is real.

What may or may not have happened within its walls are also the stuff of a mystery movie.

It was after Harrison's death in 1927 when Beaver College purchased the estate from his son and widow. And, it was soon after that when the first stories of ethereal experiences filtered through the student body and employees of the college.

The baseline of the hauntings has never been clearly established, but that fact does not diminish the intensity or integrity of the stories.

There are stories of deaths, viewings, and funeral services of Harrison family members in the "Castle," and rumors of at least two accidental deaths there.

Further, unsubstantiated tales of murder in the castle have led to such suspect notions as "indelible blood stains" that can never be washed away (which, some have said, is why the "Red Room" was painted red) and muffled screams in the middle of the night.

More plausible are the stories that revolve around the death of a little girl on a staircase in the Great Hall.

It is said that the unidentified girl was happily running down the staircase one day when her scarf somehow wrapped around a baluster, snapped her back, flipped her over the rail, snipped her spinal cord, and killed her instantly.

It is her pathetic presence that has often been felt following students and staff on the staircase. One student I spoke to claimed to have even seen the little girl's filmy form hanging from the banister. "At least," she said, "I know I saw something that looked like that."

Although she asked that I not use her name, the second-year graduate student was quite serious. "I know that I was down at the desk by the main entrance when I was distracted and saw something on the staircase. It was smoky, gray, filmy—that's the best way I can describe it. It was weird. It was small, like a little child would be, and it seemed to sway slowly, as if it was hanging over the side of the railing.

"Now," she continued, "is the really weird part. I mentioned something about it to a friend a couple hours later. She got very serious and told me I must have seen the ghost of the little girl.

"That's when I told her, and I'm telling you now, that up to that point I had never heard any story about any little girl's ghost in the Castle. I guess I was just out of the loop, but I had no idea."

So, I asked her, does she now believe what she saw could have been a ghostly image?

"Heck, I don't know," she wondered. "All I know is that I never before and never since have seen anything like it. If it was a ghost, so be it. It didn't bother me. But I do really feel for that little girl if her spirit remains there. Then again, if you have to haunt some place, it might as well be a place as beautiful as that. Is that stupid logic?"

No, young lady, it is not.

Patti Shea, a former resident assistant in the Castle, was interviewed for the *College Hauntings* video. She told the producers that students often reported unusual events during her tenure as an R.A. there.

One occasion that sticks in her memory was the time a trusted, serious student was reduced to hysteria when she awoke in her room to see, ever so faintly and briefly, the ghostly image of a man sitting silently in her room.

And then, there are the stories of the "Mirror Room," where, they say, the spirits of Mr. and Mrs. Harrison can often be seen in full formal dress, whirling away in an eternal dance.

Grey Towers looks the part and lives up to it when it comes to hauntings at Beaver College, but other buildings on campus have stories connected to them.

They say that a male ghost sprints down a hallway

and vanishes through a window at Dilworth Hall. And, "Max," the ghost, has taken up residence in Heinz Hall.

The story goes that Heinz Hall was built upon the site of a cemetery which was on the property during the Harrison years. Although careful attention was paid to remove the estimated 250 bodies from the graveyard when it was purchased by Harrison in the early 1900s, one body–Max's–was never removed and reinterred.

To this day, some students at Heinz Hall say, his angry ghost makes itself known in various ways. Telephones ring once; stereos, televisions, and microwave ovens turn themselves on–things like that.

And, there are those coeds who claim, with all sincerity, that they have awakened in the middle of the night or the middle of a nap to find a ghostly male bedmate by their side.

When they recoil and shriek in understandable fear, the interloper–Max–simply vaporizes.

Note: By the time you read this book, there is the remote chance that Beaver College may have undergone a name change. At press time, the college was polling its students for their opinions on the matter. The president of the college issued a statement that revealed a growing discontent with the name, Beaver, and its association with a particular vulgarity, the old TV show, "Leave it to Beaver," and, well, the dam-building rodents of the same name. The possibility of dropping the "Beaver" appellation came at a time the college was pursuing the possibility of seeking university status.

The Duck Pond, Haverford College

II: The Ghost on Skates

It is sometimes frustrating that I set my own firm provincial borders for the volumes in this series of books.

Often, I hear about a tantalizing ghost story, do preliminary research on it, and then realize that it takes place just over the boundary of the county which is the focus of the book.

As an example, much of the "book" research I and research partners David Seibold and Monica ("Nicki") Hartzel did for the Graeme Park story in this book came from the files of the Bucks County Historical Society and libraries there.

Until I sorted matters out, I assumed Graeme Park was in Bucks County. When I discovered that it was just over the line in Montgomery County, the story went into the "next book" file. This is what was the "next book."

I will not budge nor "fudge," however. As tempting as it may be to include a story which is set just yards over my own predetermined bounds, I will not.

Well, maybe once. Maybe for the story of the "Ghost

on Skates" at Haverford College.

But *aha!* The truth is that although the bulk of the prestigious Main Line school is in Delaware County, a central geographical setting of the "Ghost on Skates" story is actually in Montgomery.

Well, sort of. Read on.

Told and retold for generations, the story was initially collected by Charles M. Skinner, a writer for the *Brooklyn Eagle* newspaper in the latter part of the 19th century.

Among his array of stories gleaned from across the country, Skinner told the tale of the wretched wraith who took out his revenge on a Haverford student over several nights so very long ago.

Actually, this story literally crossed the county line after its very origins in Founder's Hall in the center of the college's old campus.

It was in that building, just around midnight where a fight between two students led to the demise of one and the bedevilment of the other.

Nobody's really sure how it started. It's generally accepted that a *spirit* of another kind was involved in the scuffle between the two young men.

Whatever substance may have contributed to the brawl, the end result is that after a bitter battle between the boys, one of them lay dead on the floor of the dorm room as the other–actually a friend–stood stunned.

As was reported in the initial telling of the story, it was then, at Haverford College, against regulations for one student to visit another in his dormitory room. And, it was most certainly against college rules to have alcohol on campus.

So, when he first realized what he had done–and that it was all a very tragic accident–he reckoned that he would call for help.

But while he was petrified over the killing of his classmate, the student also knew he could not easily explain the matter away.

As all sense of reason escaped from him, he concocted

a bizarre plan that would lift the burden of murder from his troubled mind.

In the corner of his room was a pair of ice skates. What if, he thought, he bundled up the corpse with an overcoat, scarf, and muffler, fitted the skates to its feet, and dragged it to the college pond?

He could find a patch of thin ice around the edge of the pond and slip the body in the water. Surely, when the lad's remains would be found it would be assumed that he had drowned.

After preparing his victim for the cover-up, the boy checked the halls. They were dark and empty.

He gripped his grim load and began the long journey to the pond.

Straining to pull the body down the corridor and staircase without being noticed, the killer froze in fear each time the skates clinked and clanged on floor, wall, or steps.

Somehow he managed to maneuver his way to the door, across the gently-sloping field along College Lane (and across into Montgomery County) to the Duck Pond.

There, he completed his clandestine deed by dumping the deceased into the pond, through the thin ice, and returning to his room.

To be sure, the student was troubled by what had happened. His conscience would never be cleared of the overwhelming guilt he must have felt.

A certain sense of relief came the next day when the victim's frozen form was discovered in the pond and word spread around campus that a young man had accidentally drowned while skating.

But soon, the dastardly deed would come back and sting the slayer's soul like a scorpion.

It was just around midnight of the day the boy's body was found in the pond.

Trying desperately to sleep, the killer lay wide-eyed in his room, reflecting on what had taken place.

At once, to his shock, he heard a sound which was all too familiar. It came from the end of the hall and headed his way.

It was the clinking and clanging sound of ice skates on floor, wall, and steps. The sound echoed lightly in the corridor, but shook the boy to his bones.

And then, he shuddered even more as slowly–ever so slowly–the knob on his dormitory door turned. The door never opened, but the knob turned.

In the otherwise silent night, a scraping sound was heard against the door.

A shadow formed at the foot of the student's bed.

From that shadow there formed a vision–the vision of a bloated, drenched man–the bloated, drenched ghost of the man who had been killed in that very room.

The apparition said nothing. It simply stared at the petrified young man in bed.

Cowering in fear and stifling sobs and screams, he tried to turn away, but the vision followed his every move.

Until, in a flash, all was once again quiet and once again dark. The ghost had gone away.

At least, that is, for that night.

After a precious few sleepless hours, he went to the college housing office and managed to have his room assignment changed. That, he was sure, would cast away at least some of the fear and guilt. After all, he reasoned, what had happened that night–the sounds, the vision–was all in his imagination.

While that thought might have consoled him for a bit, and the room change might have provided some perceived refuge, the matter would not go away that easily.

The next night, in his new room, the sounds and the vision came once more. He knew then that he could not escape the haunting.

In a crazed attempt to do so, however, the sleepless and mortified boy left the college and asked for safe haven at a friend's house in Bryn Mawr.

The friend said he would accommodate him temporarily, but the two would have to share one bed. He, of course, knew nothing about his would-be bedmate's

160

earlier transgressions.

The two men settled in for the night. Sleep came easily and soundly for the friend, but the killer was destined for another long and horrid night.

It was sometime during that night that the story took an even more shocking turn.

At the first light of dawn, the host rustled awake. He turned in bed and recoiled in absolute, uncontrollable terror.

Beside him in the bed was his guest, face up and dead.

His eyes nearly burst from their sockets.

His tongue had turned black and was bulging from his mouth.

And pressed into his neck were very distinct finger marks–marks of strangulation. Sometime in the night, at the hands of someone–or some*thing*–the killer was killed.

We know the details of this story because, it was said, that the young man revealed all while talking in his sleep.

And, while we may never really know how death was dealt to the Haverford student that night, the teller of the tale offered a final thought.

"Some say that babbling crazily in his sleep," Charles Skinner wrote, "the youth disclosed his secret and that his bedmate repeated the killing in a sort of hypnotic frenzy.

"Others believe that the drowned man's ghost returned in the small hours and avenged himself."

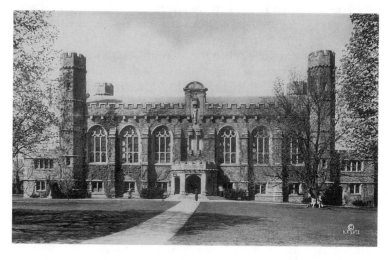

The M. Carey Thomas Library, Bryn Mawr College

III: Dr. Thomas, I Presume?

Our third campus ghost story comes from one of the most respected colleges in the United States, Bryn Mawr College.

The story comes from the pen of a distinguished author, was provided by the Bryn Mawr archivist and public relations office, and involves a pioneer feminist, champion of equal educational rights for women, first dean and second president of Bryn Mawr.

Through the years, several ghosts have been reported at several locations on the Bryn Mawr campus. One story that seems to have been lost in time is the "Bloody Pair of Eyes" or "The Red Eyes" tale that surfaced in several older compendiums of legends and lore along the Main Line.

But one account that warrants our attention is the roaming ghost of Dr. M. Carey Thomas.

During her 28 years as president of Bryn Mawr College (1894-1922), Dr. Thomas was credited with shaping the school into the superb institution it has become.

She was never one to mince words. In a scathing address at the National Suffrage Convention in 1906, Dr. Thomas cited disgraceful inequities in educational opportunities for men and women.

"Our new reform school board of Philadelphia," she said, "contains not one woman. No woman teacher receives the same salary as men teachers. Yet more than one-half of the children in the schools of Philadelphia are girls; more than nine-tenths of all the teachers are women; and it is the mothers and not the fathers who care most profoundly for the education of their children.

"I confidently believe that equal suffrage is coming far more swiftly than most of us suspect.

"Educated, public-spirited women will soon refuse to be subjected to such humiliating conditions. Educated men will recoil in their turn from the sheer unreason of the position that the opinions and wishes of their wives and mothers are to be consulted upon every other question except the laws and government under which they and their husbands and children must live and die."

Dr. Thomas was a force to be reckoned with—and may still be.

For that story, we turn to the pages of *The Making of a Feminist: Early Journals and Letters of M. Carey Thomas*, a 1980 publication of The Kent State University Press.

Edited by Marjorie Housepian Dobkin, the volume heaps high praise on Dr. Thomas. "Her influence on women's higher education," Dobkin wrote in her introduction, "by sheer force of her personality as well as more tangible achievements, is more profound than has generally been acknowledged....Carey Thomas was certainly the most compelling and dramatic figure among pioneer leaders in higher education for women."

Born to Quaker parents in Baltimore in 1857 and named Martha Carey Thomas (but called "Minnie" as a child), Dr. Thomas was described variously as "rebellious," "stubborn," and "strong-willed."

She never married, and died at age 78 in 1935.

MONTGOMERY COUNTY GHOST STORIES

Given her pertinacious character, it would be entirely believable that Dr. M. Carey Thomas's ghost might well linger on the campus she loved so dearly.

Returning to the introduction to *The Making of a Feminist*, we learn that the editor had been poring over the good doctor's papers when, she wrote, "...two of the campus guards on the night shift were reporting a ghost hovering around Canaday, the modern library building that houses the college archives."

Explaining that she often worked inside the library until around 11 o'clock at night, Dobkin continued: "According to the guards, a figure in academic robes would materialize as soon as the library lights dimmed behind me. Roving restlessly from window to window it would peer into the darkened halls of Canaday.

"It looked like, they said 'the image of the portrait' (a portrait of Carey Thomas by John Singer Sargent hangs in the M. Carey Thomas building), and when approached it would turn and vanish in the direction of the cloisters where Carey Thomas's ashes are buried–in an area of the magnificent old library building named after her."

While compiling information for this book, I spoke to two security guards at Bryn Mawr, neither of whom had any encounters with any ghosts nor even knew the story their predecessors had offered.

But, one of the guards, who asked that his name not be used, did say that the M. Carey Thomas Library, in his words, "does give me the creeps."

Does the ghost of the eminent educator really peer into the "new" library and disappear into the "old?"

Marjorie Housepian Dobkin did not discount the possibility.

It could very well be that just after the lights dim and the campus settles in for the night, the spirit–the indefatigable spirit–of Dr. Thomas watches over her beloved Bryn Mawr.

📖

The ghost of a young girl has been seen on this tower of
Hobson Hall, Ursinus College

IV: The Eerie Side of Ursinus

The folks at Ursinus College in Collegeville are rightfully proud of their venerable institution of higher learning.

Founded in 1869 by members of the German Reformed Church and co-ed since 1880, Ursinus is known to sports headline readers as a powerhouse of Division III women's sports. Two coaches of U.S. Olympic field hockey teams were Ursinus graduates.

Beyond the sports page, however, Ursinus has sent some alumni and attendees into the world as great writers

MONTGOMERY COUNTY GHOST STORIES

and scientists.

The biochemist and 1972 Nobel laureate Gerald M. Edelman is a Ursinus grad. So is Sam Keen, author of best-sellers, including *Fire in the Belly*.

The parents of Pulitzer Prize-winner and Berks County native John Updike both graduated from Ursinus in 1923. And, upon her death, Grace Hoyer Updike (who had carved out a successful career of her own as a novelist and short story writer for The New Yorker) bequeathed her literary papers to the Ursinus Library.

And then, there's a chap named J. D. Salinger, who also spent time at Ursinus–albeit only one semester–in 1938.

The academic and athletic reputation of Ursinus College thus established, there is another side of life (so to speak) on the lovely campus and in its handsome buildings.

No fewer than three dormitory and fraternity halls at Ursinus are known to hold within them ghost stories quite familiar to students there.

For those stories, we thank Jennifer Heil, a senior at Ursinus in 2000 who was kind enough to research and compile those stories.

Jen started our journey at Suite 301 in Reimert Hall, long the home of the Delta Mu Sigma fraternity and where a window-tapping wraith continually seeks entrance.

It's believed that the ghost is that of a young pledge who, several years ago was killed in a car accident.

His periodic visits to Room C of the suite have caused many students and visitors to question their own sanity.

Most often, the spirit makes its presence known by tapping on a window from the outside. When the unsuspecting resident or visitor is awakened or startled by the tapping sound, he or she will look out the window and likely catch the fleeting glimpse of a young man staring back.

In a few seconds, the image fades and vanishes.

What is truly remarkable and thought-provoking about these incidents is that the tapping is heard–and the ghostly

MONTGOMERY COUNTY GHOST STORIES

face is seen–at a window on the *third floor* of Reimert Hall!

Now, on to Shreiner Hall, one of several college-owned Victorian gems along Main Street in Collegeville.

Shreiner stands directly across from the central gates to the campus at Sixth Avenue. It once served as the college president's home but for the better part of a century has been a female dormitory.

"For years," Jennifer Heil said, "residents of the second floor complained of 'disturbances' and 'odd occurrences' going on whenever they would take a shower in the bathroom's single shower stall.

"They began as simple as weird growling noises, much like that of a defensive dog. Eventually, the residents reported that the growling became words, unintelligible at first, and finally understandable as *'get out!'* The volume of these occurrences gradually increased until the ghost was literally shouting at the bathing residents."

Ms. Heim recounted other assorted incidents, and noted that although the baseline for the haunting at Shreiner is unknown, the story of its–in her words–"extermination"– is legendary.

"Finally," she continued, "the residents decided to take action rather than continually be harassed by the ghost.

"They consulted a local priest who agreed to come to the house and perform a ceremony in their bathroom.

"With that done, the residents of Shreiner Hall were never again bothered by their ghost."

It's a different story across Sixth Avenue from Shreiner Hall, where the turret of Hobson Hall pokes into the sky above the wraparound porch and gingerbread trim of the landmark Victorian mansion.

At Hobson, the ghosts are generally harmless. Still, their presences can be disconcerting at times.

The ghosts of Hobson Hall have names: Terri and Kenny.

Again, we turn to Jennifer Heil.

"Many residents of Hobson have encountered Terri, a

167

lovely girl who died during her senior year.

"Terri sightings began occurring in the fall of 1999. One student, not a resident of Hobson Hall, was reportedly returning to his dorm late one night when he looked up to the roof of the house's tower and saw a girl sitting atop the roof, hugging her knees to her chest.

"He said the girl was a pretty blonde with very pale skin. Then, this student realized that there was no safe way for this girl to have gotten to that spot on the tower.

"He looked back up, but she was gone.

"Just before that, a resident of Hobson was staying alone in the house. It was the beginning of Fall Break and his ride could not pick him up until the day after break began. So, everybody went home and this resident was left to himself.

"He was getting ready for bed when he heard footsteps upstairs on the third floor. Thinking someone had returned to school, he went upstairs to say 'hello.' Upon inspection, he realized that no one was there.

"Back in his room, he decided to lock the door, just to be safe. Now fully awake, he began to play video games to make him sleepy again. He began to hear footsteps again, on his own floor this time. Looking out the peephole, he saw nothing. Later, during a different game, the door began to shake as though someone was trying to open it. He looked out, and again, nobody was there.

"The doorbell rang shortly afterward, with a pizza deliveryman on the other side. When the resident told him that he had not ordered a pizza, the delivery man said that order was for 586 Main Street (Hobson Hall) and that the phone number given matched this resident's room.

"After that, the resident decided to simply go to bed and ignore these strange occurrences. As he flicked off the light and climbed into the top bunk, his door suddenly began to shake, as if someone was kicking it very hard. This happened four times in succession and then stopped for the rest of the night.

"A different time, a different resident of Hobson Hall,

also alone in the house except for company in her room, reported that she and her companion, while watching a movie, began to hear footsteps throughout the rest of the house.

"Knowing that no one else was supposed to be around that night, and hearing a lot of noise coming from the bathroom next to her room, the resident decided to investigate.

"Upon opening the door to her room, she saw a blonde, pale female walk by. The girl turned to the resident and said 'hi.' The resident, who had never seen this person before either in the house or on campus, closed the door.

"After realizing that she never heard the person talking to anyone else and never heard any outside doors open or close, the resident searched the rest of the house, and found no one else around. The next day, the resident asked all of the other residents of the house, only to find that neither they, nor any of their friends, had been in the house the night before.

"Former residents of Hobson Hall report that they would be in the bathroom of the third floor, and something would turn on a faucet while they using the bathroom or flush the toilet while they would bathe. However no one had entered the bathroom during this time.

"Finally, the resident who currently lives in 'Terri's Room' reported that she will occasionally wake up in the middle of the night to see a pale, blonde girl sitting at her desk, just looking around the room.

"'Terri' is supposed to have died approximately ten years ago, in her single room on the third floor of Hobson Hall.

"After these and other odd experiences in the autumn of 1999, residents of Hobson decided to try to contact 'Terri' to see why she was causing such a commotion, and if there was any way she could be helped.

"Using a Ouija© board and gathering some believers, the group contacted Terri, who told them that she and another ghost were in the house.

"She had been seen, she said, while the other ghost, 'Kenny,' would never allow himself to be seen. Terri said that she remained in the house only because she felt that she had unfinished business on campus.

"The group also successfully contacted the 'Kenny' ghost, who told them that he was a seven-year-old boy who had died in a car accident in the street in front of the house.

"The accident happened many years before, when his mother had run the house as a boarding place for Ursinus students.

"After he died, she moved away and he was left in the house all by himself. Both spirits said that Terri now cares for Kenny, who admitted to 'playing' in the house when all or most of the residents were gone. He admitted to such things as jiggling and kicking doors."

And thus, through the mootable medium of the *Ouija*©, the ghosts of Hobson were identified.

But from the fall of 1999 until who knows how much longer, students and visitors to the lovely, old home will be on the lookout for a pale blonde girl and a playful little boy whose spirits remain in their midst.

The campus of Ursinus College as seen in a ca. 1920 post card view.

The General Wayne Inn in the early 20th century

The Ghosts of the General Wayne Inn

No book of Montgomery County ghost stories could be complete without an account of what is arguably the county's most famous ghost story of all–that of the hauntings of the General Wayne Inn.

More ink and air time has been dedicated to the General Wayne than, perhaps, any other haunted site in all of Pennsylvania.

From countless newspaper and magazine articles to books to national television segments to the internet, the General Wayne could well be called the most notorious haunted building in the Keystone State.

Many mediums, psychics, sensitives, and readers have attempted to contact or conjure up ghosts at the 625 Montgomery Ave. building–and most have succeeded.

We shall visit the latter-day General Wayne Inn as it appeared and operated while this book was being compiled. But let us first turn back time to establish the cast of ghostly characters and some possible reasons they find the General Wayne so hospitable as to stay there for eternity.

Its history is peppered with myths, mysteries, and maybes.

The General Wayne claims to be the oldest *continuously operating* restaurant in North America. While other restaurants and inns could dispute that boast–and have– there is enough evidence that meals have been served at the inn since 1704 to honor the General Wayne Inn as the only restaurant in Pennsylvania to be on the National Register of Historic Places.

It wasn't always easy to keep up that record, though. The inn closed in 1997 following an incident we will examine more closely later. There was a threat that it may not open at all in 1998, thus slicing a gap in the *continuous operation* clause and claim.

To ensure that the operation would remain technically continuous, a group called the Friends of the General Wayne Inn sponsored a lunch for local historians and preservationists. On August 10, 1998 seven people dined on $8.95 box lunches provided by a Manayunk caterer and kept the *continuity* intact.

The building has served as much more than a restaurant over the centuries. For more than 130 years, through the terms of three British kings and 19 United States presidents, the building was a post office. It was where locals voted, boarded the stage coach, bought sundries, and might have hob-nobbed with dignitaries who passed through.

Those transients may have included folks with names like Franklin (who, as postmaster general for the colonies, organized the post office in the building in 1763), Washington and Lafayette (who dined and slept there in September, 1777), Poe (who frequented the inn and is said to have scratched his initials on a window in a corner which now bears his name), or the good General Wayne himself (who dined and stayed at the inn in 1777 was later feted at the inn after his war triumphs).

172

MONTGOMERY COUNTY GHOST STORIES

Any number of generals on both sides of the Revolutionary War, signers of the Declaration of Independence, and members of the Continental Congress ate, slept, or did business within the walls of Streeper's Tavern.

Streeper's Tavern? Weren't we talking about the General Wayne Inn here?

Yes, but it was opened in 1704 by Robert Jones, and called the Wayside Inn. It eventually was purchased by Abraham Streeper, who operated it under his name to and through the Revolution. It wasn't until February 9, 1795 that the General Wayne became the General Wayne.

Maj. Gen. "Mad" Anthony Wayne and some rather rowdy troops were returning home to Pennsylvania that night and were celebrating their victory at the Battle of Fallen Timbers several months before in Ohio. They stopped at Streeper's Tavern (or, in some references, Streeper's Wayside Inn), and from the next day on, the hostelry was known as the General Wayne.

Although most of that history is basically reliable, there are incidents and episodes attributed to the General Wayne which border more on legend.

One story deals with the deaths of three Hessian mercenaries who were buried in close proximity to the inn. One of the soldiers was wounded in battle, the others were slain by a neighbor after she discovered them prowling and prying into her home.

And, it is believed that those deaths may serve as a baseline for at least some of the hauntings at the General Wayne Inn.

Ghost stories have been reported there as early as 1832, when it is documented that the innkeeper at the time, David Young, informed the Board of Elections that one official worker at the polling place that year had returned from the basement and told him that he saw the phantom figure of a Revolution-era soldier appear and disappear before his eyes.

For more than a century, several other stories of

apparitions and poltergeist activity were reported, but few were recorded.

The first "modern" report seems to date to around 1958 when a waitress told her boss that she had seen the ghost of a Hessian soldier in the same area of the basement. She later claimed to have had no knowledge of any prior ghostly sightings by others in the building.

That Hessian ghost is said to be named "Wilhelm." It is believed that upon his death, "Wilhelm" had his war medals stripped from him and taken as souvenirs, and was given an improper burial. For those reasons, his spirit now wanders within the walls of the General Wayne Inn.

And, Wilhelm is not alone–not by any stretch of the imagination.

In all, there may be as many as 17 ghosts, of both genders and all ages, races, time periods, and temperaments.

One particular ghost, the Hessian in full uniform (presumably "Wilhelm") seems to make the most frequent and frightening appearances. Numerous waitresses, waiters, and customers have seen him. Several folks have given virtually the same description of the ghost–tall, dark haired, sporting a dashing mustache, and a somewhat sly smile.

In an article written for the Valley Forge Convention & Visitors Bureau, Linda Riley recounted an interview with a former owner and manager who called one of their ethereal visitors "The Whistler."

The sound of melodic whistling–not the wind, not any other sound of nature–could be heard coming from the attic.

Disembodied footsteps and bangings on doors were often heard, as well.

And then, there was a local medium who identified more than a dozen spirits at the General Wayne. Among them were a pre-Revolution barmaid, two more Hessian soldiers, and none other than Edgar Allan Poe.

Former owner Barton Johnson, interviewed by this writer several years before research commenced for this book, gave what were probably the most credible accounts of the energies that fill the General Wayne Inn.

He told of glasses, which hung suspended from racks over the bar, that shook violently for no apparent reason. He spoke of rearranged table settings, swinging chandeliers, rapping and tapping sounds, and female customers reporting being brushed up against by unseen forces.

Some employees there have asked not to be assigned to certain areas. Conversely, some workers (and many patrons) *prefer* to venture into the most haunted areas in hopes of having an "experience."

Old "Wilhelm" might have some very close and perhaps familiar company in the form of "Max," "Hans," and "Ludwig," three other Hessian soldiers whose ghosts remain at the inn, according to other mediums who read the building in the 1980s.

Those individuals met several spirits there. A young woman–invisible to most folks–tends the main bar from time to time.

A black man's ghost wanders in and out of the kitchen, and an Indian glides through walls, sits at booths, and has been seen in shadowy, filmy form in the ladies' room.

Those, then, are the ghosts of restaurants *past* at the General Wayne Inn.

In the years leading up to publication of this book, much has happened on many fronts at the local landmark.

On December 27, 1996, former inn co-owner James Webb was found shot to death in his third-floor office there. Two months later, an assistant chef committed suicide, and a knot of intrigue continued to tangle as the restaurant–deep in debt and falling into steady disrepair–remained closed.

At press time, Webb's murder was still unsolved.

But, the fortunes of the inn took a turn for the better when two eager and experienced Philadelphia restaurateurs purchased the site and pumped new life into the old inn.

Although it took some rather daring and historically discomfiting changes to make the business viable in a very

175

competitive environment, the General Wayne reopened.

One thing that did *not* change was the haunted heritage of the inn.

Let us now examine the ghosts of restaurant *present* at the General Wayne Inn.

Those ghosts continue to draw both novice and experienced ghost hunters to the General Wayne for closer looks.

Such was the case when a nine-member team from the Philadelphia Ghost Hunters Alliance conducted an investigation of the inn.

Armed with electromagnetic field detectors, digital cameras and other equipment, the PGHA members spread out through the entire building in search of the anomalies and energy field aberrations that may indicate levels of spirit activity.

What did they find? One member recorded wild levels of electromagnetic field (EMF) levels, but dismissed them as the result of a large number of generators, machinery, and utilities inside the General Wayne's basement.

Others photographed so-called "orbs," or globular images which they and the ghost-hunting community believe can indicate a high concentration of psychic energy.

One member managed to squeeze into a cramped space in the basement and, according to a report filed for the PGHA archives, "I caught a small streak of white light shoot off to my left. It was only there for a second. There was no way an outside source could have caused that without me knowing. There is only one way to get to that room and it was past me."

That same member later claimed to have heard a sigh coming from that tight basement space as he prepared to leave it. "It was a woman's sigh, to be more specific. I immediately felt that she was sad to see me go. That feeling came out of nowhere."

Another member (PGHA investigators post their reports publicly using only their first name and initial of their surname) did say she felt as if she saw what she described as a "misty form of some sort" appear in the George Washington Room of the inn.

Still another detected slight, long-term movement in groupings of silverware in that same room.

But, when the preliminary individual reports were filed, the PGHA jury was still out.

A senior investigator noted, "I personally found no evidence that supports the claim of a spirit and/or haunting activity at the General Wayne (at least not now). However, I do know that many, many people have witnessed the Inn's many ghosts on numerous occasions. So, based on the GWI's history and the many stories told by Merion's residents, I cannot say for sure as to whether or not the inn is haunted or not. If I had to go on my findings alone I would say it is not."

However, each did agree that there was far too much human hubbub going on while their investigations were being conducted. That energy may well have interfered and muted the spirit activity.

To a member, they agreed that further, deeper, and quieter investigations should and would be made.

Certainly in the time between those initial probes and the time you are reading this book, those investigations have been made. And certainly, considering the haunted heritage of the General Wayne, the scant but significant anomalies detected by the PGHA, and the assiduous reports of ghostly activity from staff members and customers of the inn, America's oldest continuously operating *restaurant* will be among the country's oldest continuously operating *haunted* restaurants.

Do ghosts haunt an American historical shrine?

Ghosts of Valley Forge

It is a site of the sacrifice of thousands of soldiers who suffered unimaginable conditions during the winter of 1777-78.

It is where a true, professional American army was born, where alliances were formed, and where leaders gained the confidence they would need for the struggle which was to follow.

And, although there was no battle fought there, it is where an estimated two to three thousand men perished from exposure and disease.

It is Valley Forge, and it is a *bona fide* American historical shrine.

We began this book with what was hailed as "America's *First* Ghost Story"—the story of one innocent farm girl whose encounter with the unknown vaulted her name into the history books. So, it is fitting that we will conclude with what could well be America's *greatest* ghost story, attributed to America's first president, and set in Valley Forge, Montgomery County, Pennsylvania.

MONTGOMERY COUNTY GHOST STORIES

Is Valley Forge haunted?

The National Park Service, which oversees the National Historical Park, will not say. Its historians deal only with indisputable, irrefutable facts. Legends are too gray for their black-or-white world of history.

And, so be it.

So, the park service was little help while tracking down the ghost stories of Valley Forge. But, be assured, there are ghosts there.

Several people, from casual and unsuspecting tourists to park guards and maintenance workers, have reported hearing, seeing, and sensing spirits there.

The ghosts of Colonial soldiers have been detected in and near the earthworks and huts at Valley Forge. Several credible photographs of these entities have been taken, and some have been published.

And, while those in tune with the "other side" note that most of the spirits in the park are those of enlisted men, at least two very illustrious entities have made their presences known there.

Baron von Steuben and Gen. George Washington have apparently left eternal imprints at Valley Forge. One psychic claims Washington's spirit energy is strongest at the stone house which served as his headquarters.

Von Steuben's ghost has been spotted along the Schuylkill River near the old Valley Forge railroad station.

These stories remain nebulous, however.

Certain documents do confirm that in 1895, quite a sensation was created when several individuals reported seeing the spirits of Revolutionary War-era soldiers strolling between glowing campfires on the ridges of what is now the national park.

Perhaps as a tribute to those sacrifices made at Valley Forge by those Americans so very long ago, we should allow these and other stories there to rest in that "gray zone" of history. Perhaps this American historical shrine should remain inviolable–its ghosts invisible forever.

Again, so be it.

But, as we alluded to earlier in this chapter, there is one ghost story, of a sort, which has been placed in Valley Forge and cannot be ignored.

Gray zone or no gray zone, that story must be included here.

It has been printed and re-printed in journals, magazines, newspapers, and now on the Internet since it was first released to a national readership in the Civil War veterans' newspaper *The National Tribune* (which evolved into *The Stars and Stripes©*).

In December, 1880, the *Tribune* presented to its readers, to America, and to posterity, a story of wondrous patriotic and paranormal proportions.

The account, said to have been found in private documents as early as 1861 and published privately in 1865, has nonetheless been resoundingly rebuffed by scholars and those "black-or-white" historians.

But, even they have not been able to totally disprove its authenticity. In fact, one researcher did discover that the teller of the tale repeatedly affirmed its veracity until the day he died.

That teller was none other than George Washington. The tale has gone down in history–albeit the *gray zone* of history–as "Washington's Vision at Valley Forge."

The story was handed down by Anthony Sherman, who claimed to have been at Valley Forge during the historic winter encampment.

Sherman told his story to a respected Philadelphia journalist named Wesley Bradshaw. Bradshaw wrote in his preface to the "Vision" that he had met the 99-year old Sherman in 1859 in Independence Square, Philadelphia.

After they exchanged smalltalk for a bit, Sherman said to Bradshaw, "I want to tell you of an incident of George Washington's life, one which no one alive knows of except myself."

This is that incident, in the words of Anthony Sherman and from the pen of Wesley Bradshaw.

You have doubtless heard the story of Washington's going

180

to the thicket to pray. Well, it was not only true, but he used often to pray in secret for aid and comfort from God, the interposition of whose Divine Providence brought us safely through the darkest days of tribulation.

One day, I remember well, the chilly winds whistled through the leafless trees, though the sky was cloudless and the sun shone brightly, he remained in his quarters nearly all the afternoon alone. When he came out, I noticed that his face was a shade paler than usual, and there seemed to be something on his mind of more than ordinary importance. Returning just after dusk, he dispatched an orderly to the quarters of the officer I mention who was presently in attendance. After a preliminary conversation of about half an hour, Washington, gazing upon his companion with that strange look of dignity which he alone could command said to the latter:

'I do not know whether it is owing to anxiety of my mind, or what, but this afternoon, as I was sitting at this table engaged in preparing a dispatch, something seemed to disturb me. Looking up, I beheld standing opposite me a singularly beautiful female. So astonished was I, for I had given strict orders not to be disturbed, that it was some moments before I found language to inquire the cause of her presence. A second, a third, and even a fourth time did I repeat my question, but received no answer from my mysterious visitor except a slight raising of her eyes.

'Presently I heard a voice saying, "Son of the Republic, look and learn," while at the same time my visitor extended her arm eastwardly. I now beheld a heavy white vapor at some distance rising fold upon fold. This gradually dissipated, and I looked upon a strange scene. Before me lay spread out in one vast plain all the countries of the world–Europe, Asia, Africa, and America. I saw rolling and tossing, between Europe and America, the billows of the Atlantic, and between Asia and America lay the Pacific.

'"Son of the Republic," said the same mysterious voice as before, "look and learn." At that moment I beheld a dark, shadowy being, like an angel, standing, or rather floating, in the hollow air, between Europe and America. Dipping water out of the ocean in the hollow of each hand, he sprinkled some upon

181

America with his right hand while with his left hand he cast some on Europe. Immediately a cloud raised from these countries and joined in mid-ocean. For a while it remained stationary, and then moved slowly westward, until it enveloped America in its murky folds. Sharp flashes of lightning gleamed through it at intervals, and I heard the smothered groans and cries of the American people.

'A second time the angel dipped water from the ocean, and sprinkled it out as before. The dark cloud was then drawn back to the ocean, in whose heaving billows it sank from view. A third time I heard the mysterious voice saying, "Son of the Republic, look and learn." I cast my eyes upon America and beheld villages and towns and cities springing up one after another until the whole land, from the Atlantic to the Pacific, was dotted with them. Again I head the mysterious voice say, "Son of the Republic, the end of the century cometh, look and learn."

'At this the dark shadowy angel turned his face southward, and from Africa I saw an ill-omened spectre approach our land. It flitted slowly over every town and city of the latter. The inhabitants presently set themselves in battle array against each other. As I continued looking, I saw a bright angel, on whose brow rested a crown of light, on which was traced the word "Union," bearing the American flag which he placed between the divided nation, and said, "Remember ye are brethren." Instantly, the inhabitants casting from them their weapons became friends once more, and united around the National Standard.

'And again I heard the mysterious voice saying, "Son of the Republic, look and learn." At this, the dark, shadowy angel placed a trumpet to his mouth and blew three distinct blasts; and taking water from the ocean, he sprinkled it upon Europe, Asia, and Africa. Then my eyes beheld a fearful scene. From each of these countries arose thick, black clouds that were soon joined into one. And throughout this mass, there gleamed a dark red light by which I saw hordes of armed men, who, moving with the cloud, marched by land and sailed by sea to America, which country was enveloped in the volume of cloud. And I *dimly saw these vast armies devastate the whole country, and burn the villages, towns and cities that I beheld springing up.*

'As my ears listened to the thundering of the cannon, clashing of swords, and the shouts and cries of millions in mortal combat, I again heard the mysterious voice saying, "Son of the Republic, look and learn." When the voice had ceased, the dark shadowy angel placed his trumpet once more to his mouth, and blew a long and fearful blast.

'Instantly a light as of a thousand suns shone down from above me, and pierced and broke into fragments the dark cloud which enveloped America. At the same moment the angel upon whose head still shone the word "Union," and who bore our national flag in one hand and a sword in the other, descended from the heavens attended by legions of white spirits. These immediately joined the inhabitants of America, who I perceived were well-nigh overcome, but who immediately taking courage again closed up their broken ranks and renewed the battle. Again, amid the fearful noise of the conflict, I heard the mysterious voice saying, "Son of the Republic, look and learn."

'As the voice ceased, the shadowy angel for the last time dipped water from the ocean and sprinkled it upon America. Instantly the dark cloud rolled back, together with the armies it had brought, leaving the inhabitants of the land victorious.

'Then once more I beheld the villages, towns and cities, springing up where I had seen them before, while the bright angel, plating the azure standard he had brought in the midst of them, cried with a loud voice: "While the stars remain, and the heavens send down dew upon the earth, so long shall the Union last." And taking from his brow the crown on which was blazoned the word "Union," he placed it upon the Standard, while the people, kneeling down, said "Amen."

'The scene instantly began to fade and dissolve, and I at last saw nothing but the rising, curling vapor I at first beheld. This also disappearing, I found myself once more gazing upon the mysterious visitor, who in the same voice I had heard before, said, "Son of the Republic, what you have seen is thus interpreted. Three great perils will come upon the Republic. The

183

most fearful is the third."

'With these words the vision vanished, and I started from my seat and felt that I had seen a vision wherein had been shown me the birth, progress, and destiny of the UNITED STATES.'

Was this the concoction of an ambitious journalist? Was it the rambling of an old man? Did it really ever happen?

Or, was it an accurate, if aggrandized, account of a series of ghostly, angelic, or–as some observers have offered–extra-terrestrial visitations on the man who would be this nation's first president?

Whatever the case, it remains as one of the most mystical and mysterious stories to emerge from the seminal years of the United States.

And, truth or fiction, it happened in Montgomery County.

About the Author

This is the 22nd book by Charles J. Adams III. His other efforts focused mainly on ghost stories and legends, but have also included volumes on maritime disasters and trainwrecks.

Adams was born in Reading, Pennsylvania, in 1947 and resides there today. In addition to his books, Adams also writes regular features on travel and local legends in the *Reading Eagle* newspaper and has written travel stories for several other magazines and publications.

He is also the host of the morning show, "Charlie & Company" on WEEU / 830AM in Reading.

In constant demand as a speaker, Adams has been a keynote speaker at the International Ghost Hunters Alliance conventions in Gettysburg, Pa., and has been interviewed on ghostly topics in England, Ireland, South Africa, and on several American radio and television stations.

He has also appeared on The History Channel's "Haunted America: New York" episode and has organized and escorted tours of haunted places in the United States, England, and Scotland.

His stories have been selected for inclusion in such books as "Classic American Ghost Stories" (August House Publishing) and "HexCraft" (Llewellyn Publications).

A singer in rock bands since his high school days, Adams has also written numerous commercial jingles and songs, and several have been recorded and released on CDs and music videos.

Adams has served as president of the board of trustees of the Reading, Pennsylvania Public Library, a school director in the Exeter Township School District, and as a member of the board of directors of the Historical Society of Berks County, the Penn State Alumni Society of the Berks Campus, and the Exeter Community Library. Listed in "Who's Who in American Entertainment," Adams has been honored several times for his civic work in his home town.

Among his many accomplishments he lists among his personal favorites his singing, *a capella*, of the National Anthem before several Reading Phillies minor league baseball games.

MONTGOMERY COUNTY GHOST STORIES

Acknowledgments

NEWSPAPERS & BOOKS

1877 Atlas of Montgomery County (J.D. Scott); Pottstown Mercury, History of Montgomery County, Pennsylvania, Illustrated, 1884 (Theodore W. Bean); Main Line Times, Reading Eagle-Times, The Main Line Chronicle, Norristown Times Herald, The Ghostly Register (Arthur Myers), A History of Pottstown, 1752-1952, Philadelphia Inquirer, Philadelphia Evening Bulletin, Montgomery Lifestyles, The Bulletin of the Historical Society of Montgomery County, Limerick Township: A Journey Through Time 1699-1987 (Muriel E. Lichtenwalner), The Goschenhoppen Region, Doylestown Daily Intelligencer, National Enquirer, Local Sketches and Legends, 1887 (William J. Buck), Cheltenham Tri-Centennial, 1690-1990, The Recorder, The Making of a Feminist, Edited by Marjorie Housepian Dobkin; Antiques magazine, Philadelphia magazine, Philadelphia Weekly, The Valley Item, A Compendium of the History of Upper Frederick Township

ORGANIZATIONS

Historical Society of Montgomery County, Lower Merion Historical Society, Lower Merion Library System, Upper Merion Township Library, Old York Road Historical Society, SEPTA, Valley Forge Convention and Visitors Bureau, Upper Moreland Historical Assn., Goschenhoppen Historians, Abington Parks & Recreation Dept., Upper Perkiomen Valley Chamber of Commerce, Montgomery County Department of History & Cultural Arts, Valley Forge National Historical Park, Pennsylvania Historical and Museum Commission, Pottstown Public Library, Reading Public Library, Valley Forge Historical Society, Philadelphia Ghost Hunters Alliance, Schwenksville Bicentennial Committee, Norristown Library, Lower Merion Conservancy, Pottstown Historical Society, Historical Society of Berks County, Library of Congress

INDIVIDUALS

Dave Seibold, Monica Hartzel, Terri Adams, Debbi Kerr, Kimberly Pikunis, Debbie Parkins, Clara P. Hoss, Doug Heller, Chris Hagner, John Cottingham, Linda L. Riley, Jennifer Bolognese, Sally Widman, Ray Stahl, Nancy Collins, Betty Wlazelek, Deborah Merritt, Sue Habgood, Mike Zuckerman, Ted Goldsborough, Linda Manz, Lorett Treese, Katharine Schweriner

...and countless others whose pleasant paths we crossed. Thanks to all, and sincere apologies to anyone we overlooked.

📖

ALSO FROM EXETER HOUSE BOOKS

INCE
982...

LISHERS

OF

JALITY

OOKS

ON

KLORE

AND

GENDS

N THE

ATLANTIC

TATES

BUCKS COUNTY GHOST STORIES

PHILADELPHIA GHOST STORIES

NEW YORK CITY GHOST STORIES

CAPE MAY GHOST STORIES, BOOK I

CAPE MAY GHOST STORIES, BOOK II

SHIPWRECKS & LEGENDS 'ROUND CAPE MAY

POCONO GHOSTS, LEGENDS & LORE, BOOK I

POCONO GHOSTS, LEGENDS & LORE, BOOK II

GHOST STORIES OF PITTSBURGH AND ALLEGHENY COUNTY

PENNSYLVANIA DUTCH COUNTRY GHOSTS, LEGENDS & LORE

GHOST STORIES OF THE LEHIGH VALLEY

GHOST STORIES OF THE DELAWARE COAST

GHOST STORIES OF BERKS COUNTY, BOOK I

GHOST STORIES OF BERKS COUNTY, BOOK II

GHOST STORIES OF BERKS COUNTY, BOOK III

BERKS THE BIZARRE

LEGENDS OF LONG BEACH ISLAND

SHIPWRECKS OFF OCEAN CITY (N.J.)

GREAT TRAIN WRECKS OF EASTERN PENNSYLVANIA

THE NEW YORK CITY FIRE PATROL:

AN ILLUSTRATED HISTORY

JOE'S BOYS: THE STORY OF THE FERKO STRING BAND

OF PHILADELPHIA

ALL

TITLES

AVAILABLE

AT BOOK

STORES

and

MAJOR

ONLINE

BOOKSELLERS

OR A FREE CATALOG AND MAIL ORDER INFORMATION WRITE TO
EXETER HOUSE BOOKS, P.O. BOX 8134, READING, PA 19603
ExHouseBoo@aol.com   David J. Seibold, Publisher